Ron
Mâsak

I've Met All My Heroes from A

Published in the USA by:
BearManor Media
PO Box 1129
Duncan, Oklahoma 73534-1129
www.bearmanormedia.com

ISBN 978-1-59393-510-8

Printed in the United States of America.
Book design by Brian Pearce | Red Jacket Press.

Table of Contents

Foreword

I was a street kid from Chicago, raised right in the heart of the city and in the shadow of Comiskey Park, home of the White Sox. This street kid grew up to play golf with three men who had walked on the moon, skied with another astronaut and played tennis with still another. The general who commanded Desert Storm drove me around for a week as we shot sporting clays. I got to hang out with the greatest pilot in history and mingle with names out of the history books.

One of those names was the legendary Vince Lombardi, with whom I starred in the most-seen, non-theatrical film in history, *Second Effort*. Ever the athlete and baseball lover, I was issued a uniform and worked out for 20 years with the Los Angeles Dodgers. In the world of politics, I spent one-on-one time with five United States presidents. I had the privilege of starring in three videos with Hall of Fame golfers and have emceed thousands of shows with Hall of Famers from every walk of life. As an actor/entertainer, I have been allowed to tour the world and work, play and socialize with some of the all-time icons of the entertainment, political and sports worlds. Perhaps my best-known role was that of Sheriff Mort Metzger on television's most successful mystery show, *Murder, She Wrote*, which is still in syndication worldwide.

For many, these experiences might be considered the very best life could offer, but my greatest blessing of all was to marry my Kay, one of the truly great ladies of the world who gave me six incredible children. They, in turn, have given me five granddaughters, one grandson and a life richer than I ever dreamed of in those early days in Chicago. Here then, are just some of those moments with some of those people, relived. They are my heroes and I hope that by the time you have finished this book, at least some of them will be yours, too.

All the best always, in all ways!

Ron Mâsak

To My Kay:
Who gave me the greatest treasures a man can have…
Family, Love, Respect, Laughter.

"Hero — A person noted for feats of courage or *nobility of purpose*."

Merriam-Webster Dictionary

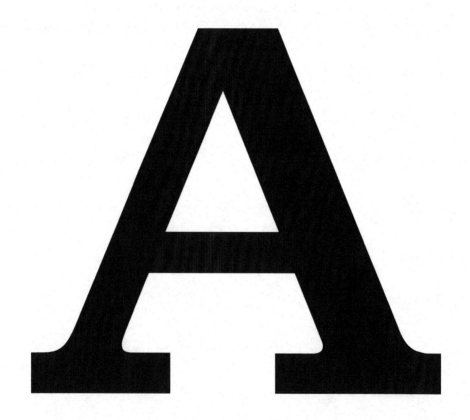

Buzz Aldrin

Buzz and I met at a celebrity charity event, and over the years, we have done many together: golf, tennis and skiing. He is a wonderful storyteller and a good athlete. While many humorous anecdotes come to mind, one that stands out in my mind is the year I emceed a Navy dinner dance honoring Buzz and Rod Steiger. It was a black-tie affair at the Beverly Hilton Hotel and during the dinner our host was getting very concerned, as neither of the honored guests had arrived as yet.

Halfway through dinner, Rod arrived and apologized for being late. It seems there was another dinner event being held at the hotel and he wound up there, but halfway through his meal, he realized that he was at the wrong affair. So he hurried to the right room, apologized and proceeded to enjoy his second meal.

Now Buzz is another story. Coffee and dessert were being served and still no Buzz except for the one in the room, wondering where he was. I suggested to our host that perhaps someone should go check the other party to see if Buzz made the same mistake Rod had made. A scouting party went out and returned unsuccessfully, so time to get on with the show and the presentations. By this time our host and his committee were furious. Many calls were made to Buzz, but no answer. As the event ended and I said my goodbyes, my wife Kay and I were leaving the ballroom and heading for the lobby of the hotel when we

looked up and saw Lois and Buzz Aldrin in full military dress uniform…slowly striding toward the ballroom we just left. Kay wanted to know if we should say something or go back; 80 percent of the audience was gone by now but 20 percent had stayed to dance. I declined, though it would have been interesting to hear how a man who could find his way to the moon could get lost on his way to the Beverly Hilton Hotel.

Steve Allen

Perhaps the only *true* all around genius in the history of show business. Steve could do it *all*. Talk Show pioneer (he was the original host of *The Tonight Show*) Best selling author, playwright, actor, comedian, poet, he starred in movies, Television, Nightclubs, Theatre, the lecture circuit and on and on. Steve composed over 7900 songs. Andy Williams once said of him that "Steve is the only man to be listed on *all* the yellow pages. He use to carry a small tape recorder wherever he went as whenever an idea hit him for any project out it came. He was always kind enough to appear for me on the Jerry Lewis MDA telethon that I hosted locally for many years. One time we were at a social function and as he and his lovely wife Jayne Meadows came to join us at our table I said. "Well Steve have you written a song since you got here?"

Out came the recorder. What a guy.

Muhammad Ali

I was blessed to emcee a number of events where The Champ was the guest of honor. Ali is one of the most giving and recognizable men on the face of the earth. He was a great fighter and fought the best heavyweights around and he just may have been, as he boasted, The Greatest of All Time. At a dinner for

Roxy Campanella, widow of 3-time MVP Hall of Fame Brooklyn Dodger, Roy Campanella, Ali sat in that ballroom for hours after the dinner to sign an autograph for *everyone*.

I remembered the first time we had met. It was in the green room of the *Joey Bishop Show*. He had recently been stripped of his Championship title when he refused to be inducted into the Army. He was sitting with four members of the Black Muslims, who were very somber. It was so *very* quiet, so I piped up with, "Hey, I just thought of a way to make headlines overnight and become famous… 'Unknown actor punches Heavyweight Champion of the world.'" He laughed but the four somber men immediately stood up as if to protect him. I smiled and said, "Oh sit down. I'm from Chicago and if I were going to do something like that, I would have hit him and *then* announced it." As I said it, Ali laughed and had them sit.

One of my favorite stories about the Champ took place at Dodger Stadium in the old dugout seats. He was there with his friend and biographer, Howard Bingham. I walked over to the edge of the dugout and got manager Tommy Lasorda's attention to let him know Ali was there. Tommy asked me to bring Ali over, so I walked back to the Champ and said, "Tommy would like you to come over and say hello to the team."

His response was, "Will he give me a couple of hats?"

"Hats?" I said, "He'll give you hats, balls, bats and if you want to play first base, he would probably let you do it." A gracious Ali went over and teased the team for a few minutes. He lit up that dugout where major leaguers, who normally were not easily impressed, were just like the rest of the world…in awe of "The Greatest of All Time." By the way, he did get all of the above except for playing first base.

Neil Armstrong

We were doing a celebrity golf tournament in Florida and there he was, the first man to step on the moon. A shy and humble man, he had been used to hearing word for word the same thing when he was introduced to someone, "I can tell you exactly where I was and what I was doing when you stepped on the moon." He had heard that for years and yet would smile graciously. Why would he care what a stranger was doing, yet he smiled. Well, when I was introduced to him and he primed himself to hear those words, he didn't. I said instead, "Ever since you brought that rock back from the moon, our weather has been shit." He exploded with laughter and every time we saw each other that weekend, he would call me over to repeat what I said. This is a wonderful and gracious hero. The following year we did the same event and once again he would call me over to relate the story. See — he never forgot where *he* was or what *he* was doing when he met *me!*

Neil Armstrong.

Joe Arpaio

Joe Arpaio, Sheriff of Mariposa County in Arizona, had a book written about him called *America's Toughest Sheriff*. My wife and I were attending a charity event in Arizona a few summers ago. We were at a western outdoor barbecue, *Murder, She Wrote* was a top-ten show nationwide, and I was riding a high wave of being recognized.

I was approached by a man who said, "How would you like to meet America's toughest sheriff?" I answered, "You mean America's *second* toughest sheriff?" He laughed and said, "Oh, is Joe going to like you." So I was brought over to meet Sheriff Joe — the man who keeps prisoners in tents and pink underwear, has male and female chain gangs, and doesn't let his prisoners read girlie magazines or lift weights.

When we were introduced, he said to me, "I hear you are famous." I asked his definition of fame. He said, "Well, I'm famous. They wrote a book about me and I have been on shows like *Larry King*."

"Oh, well, if that's the criteria," I responded, "and since *Murder, She Wrote* is seen in countries *all over the world* in *many* languages, I guess I *am* famous."

After that, we got along *famously*. You either like or dislike Joe Arpaio; there is no middle ground. His enemies hate him and his friends believe in what he does. While we were talking, a reporter came over and asked Joe if he didn't think it was cruel and inhumane to keep prisoners in tents in the heat of Arizona. Joe answered, "We had young fighting men and women in Desert Storm living in tents with twice the heat of Arizona and never saw one thing about that in your paper." That was the end of that conversation. Over the years we have stayed in touch and I have emceed charity affairs with him. He told *Entertainment Tonight* that if they ever do a movie about him, he wants me to play the role. I am ready!

Fred Astaire

I have always admired the great dancers in the movies, as I always felt that they were truly the best athletes: Mr. Astaire, Gene Kelly, Donald O'Connor, The Nicholas Brothers, Dan Dailey, Ann Miller, and Debbie Reynolds, among others. They could play on my team anytime.

One day in the early '70s, I was in a Beverly Hills parking lot. At that time I had a Mercedes 450 SL and was putting the top down. I got in and started to pull out when, about 50 yards away, I saw a man walking away with a most familiar and distinctly recognizable gait…and I immediately knew it could only belong to Fred Astaire. I have never been one to bother a celebrity, and had no intention of starting then, but I just *had* to say hello. So, I pulled up alongside and said, "Mr. Astaire, I don't wish to bother you but I just wanted to say thank you for all the years of joy and entertainment you have given me and the rest of the world." He smiled and leaned over into my car and with that delightful twinkle in his eye said, "Well, thank you and may I say that I enjoy your work, too...*Ron*." I froze. Fred Astaire knew my name and I beamed as he walked to his car. It was I, not he, who was dancing...on air.

Gene Autry

Gene is affectionately known as "The Cowboy." I first met Gene in the late 1950s at a place called Jimmy Cox Keith's Café in Studio City. Jimmy was Tex Ritter's manager and owned this club and until I opened there it was all western. I was opening the night Tex Williams and the Whippoorwills were closing. The guest list included Johnny Cash, Jimmy Wakely, Marty Robbins, Lefty Frizzell, Spade Cooley and The Cowboy.

Before I went on, they asked Gene to sing. He did and despite being in the month of July, he finished with his biggest selling record. He sang, "You know Dasher and Dancer and Comet and Blitzen…" Yes, *Rudolph the Red-Nosed Reindeer* in July.

And then I was on. In those days, I was doing impressions and opened with a few Bobby Darin numbers and closed with a lot of Elvis. Gene turned to Spade Cooley, who had a live weekly television show, and said, "Put that boy on this Saturday's show." He did and I am forever grateful.

Over the years I was privileged to emcee many shows for Gene and many where he was on the dais. On time in particular was for the Masquers' Dinner honoring Ben Johnson. The dais included Sam Peckinpah, Jane Russell, Richard Brooks, Steven Ford, the President's son, and The Cowboy. I gave him what he always told me was the greatest introduction he ever received, and he came to the mike and stared at me for what I felt was an eternity. I thought to myself, "Oh my God, he is up and forgot what he was going to say." Wrong, Mâsak! He looked at me and said, "You think I don't know, huh, Ron? You think I don't know."

"What's that, Cowboy?" I responded.

"You think I don't know that you hang out with Tommy Lasorda every night at Dodger Stadium [Gene owned The California Angels]. You all know Tommy… the only man who can belly up to a bar *before* he enters the room." He was on a roll with material the great Pat Buttram wrote for him that night. (Pat was his sidekick in movies and on television and a funny man.)

Gene Autry.

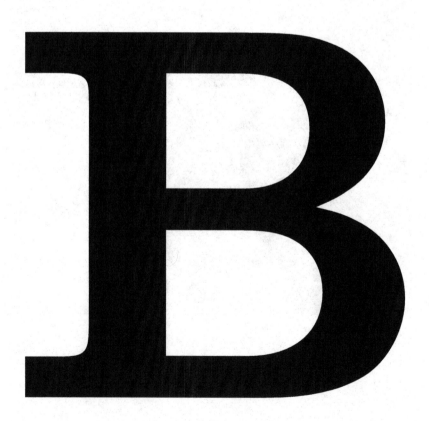

Lucille Ball

I had met Lucy and been with her at a number of events and she was always so kind and encouraging to me. *I Love Lucy* has *never* been off the air...and is still funnier than most of what we see now. Former Green Bay Packer star and author Jerry Kramer and his wife came to visit one day and asked if they could meet Lucy so I took them over to Stage 25 at Universal Studios (where years later the Sheriff of Cabot Cove's office would be), where they

met Lucy. Instead of motor homes, Lucy, and her then-husband, Gary Morton, built a little community on the soundstage itself. She invited us into her bungalow. This gracious icon spent the next two hours talking to them, answering questions and telling stories. Here was this Hall of Fame right guard from the Super Bowl Champions in total awe of this great star. Any wonder why to this day people still say, "I Love Lucy"?

Jack Benny

George Burns said that his friend, Jack Benny, had the greatest timing of anyone in the history of show business; that he could wait for five minutes and know the laugh would come. He was also Burns' greatest audience. Burns could say, "Hello," and Jack would crack up.

One year, a charitable group of Ladies known as SHARE, had Jack headline the show with a nostalgic trip down memory lane about Benny growing up in Waukegan, Illinois. The gala was a sellout and not open to the public, so great stars did things to entertain that few people ever got to see on the screen.

On stage as Jack went door to door on his trip, Rock Hudson would open a door and sing and dance with Nancy Walker, Lucille Ball would open the next one and do a skit, Jack Lemmon, Milton Berle and Edie Adams revived one of the Great Ernie Kovacs' classics, The Nairobi Trio, etc. After the show, we had an opportunity to say hello and what a charming man he was. His singer on the show was Dennis Day. Dennis' brother, Dr. James McNulty (married to movie star Ann Blyth, with whom I did an episode of *Quincy*), was Kay's OB.

Well. Jack, God love him, passed away on December 26, 1974. Twenty-six hours later, our twin sons, Mike and Bob, were being delivered by Dr. McNulty, and I kid you not...when I went to look at them, one of them had his little face cuddled in his hand the same way Jack Benny would cup his face.

I should point out here that Dr. M was one of my heroes as well. In those days, fathers weren't allowed in delivery unless they went through some classes. Well, while Dr. M was scrubbing up, he told me to wait. A nurse right out of the Nurse Ratched (the nurse in *One Flew Over the Cuckoo's Nest*) school told me I must wait in the father's waiting room until the babies came. I informed her that I was going to be in the delivery room. She sternly looked at me and said, "Oh, have you been to Lamaze class?"

I answered, "No, but I know how to breathe."

When Dr. M came in, she looked at him as though I wasn't even in the building and said, "Oh, Doctor, is the father going to be *allowed* in the delivery room?"

He didn't miss a beat. He replied, "He wouldn't miss it for the world," threw me my greens and off we went. My boys were born in two different rooms in two different ways. Mike came quickly and naturally and then an hour later, with the spinal wearing off, it was decided a Caesarian was needed and they moved Kay to the OR and Bob was born. Talk about Jack Benny and *timing*…Wow!!!

Ingrid Bergman

In the late '60s, I was doing a lot of work on the Columbia Studios lot, and when I had time, I would sneak onto other sets and watch the filming. They were shooting *Cactus Flower* and I went over to watch one of the great actresses of *all time*, Ingrid Bergman. All movie stars were bigger than life to me, but this lady was one of my all-time favorites, so I went to watch…and learn. She had a magnificent look about her, classic beauty with little need for makeup, and a great stride when she walked.

My Bergman story is short and sweet. She was walking in a darkened area of the soundstage where I happened to be watching from, and as she was walking something distracted her. She started to trip over a cable box and I caught her. She smiled, kissed me on the cheek and thanked me…so from that moment on, I can honestly tell the world that I held Ingrid Bergman in my arms.

Julius Boros

One of the all-time great Hall of Fame golfers. I starred in a motivational film with him and Jay, as he was called, was the Perry Como/Dean Martin of the links — totally laid back and relaxed. He wrote a book on golf entitled *Swing Easy, Hit Hard*. When I arrived in Florida and went to the course to meet him, he said, "Let's go hit a bucket of balls and get loose." I hit about ten balls and he looked over at me and said, "You have bursitis in your right shoulder and still play baseball?" He knew all of that from ten swings of the club…and he was right.

Jay and Armen had a large family and she and I still stay in touch at Christmas. I spent a lovely few days with him and he said the most profound thing I ever heard about golf, but it wasn't used in the film. He said, "Anyone who shoots

golf in the hundreds consistently has no business on a golf course…and anyone who shoots in the seventies…*has no business.*"

Marlon Brando

Yes, *that* Marlon Brando. In 1955, our college theatre group would go to New York during Easter vacation. We would see some plays and go backstage to meet the stars…some really great experiences for another time. But Karl Malden's brother, Danny Sekulovich, was a good friend of our director and of Marlon. My director, knowing that I was serious about pursuing an acting career and knowing that I was a Brando worshiper, set up a luncheon meeting in the Grill of The Taft Hotel where we all stayed. He showed up and I  was in awe. He was shorter than I thought but had a great smile. And, he was fun to be with. We would do impressions and he was good. He did a wonderful Claude Rains, which if you listen carefully you can hear him do in *Desiree*. He ordered a beer which he did not drink but used to dunk those miniature hot dogs in.

The whole time we were there, three ladies in a nearby booth kept staring holes in him. As they saw we were getting ready to leave and they had been finished for a good 15 minutes beforehand, they started to make their move. Marlon whipped around and said, "May I be of help to you ladies?" They giggled and squirmed, telling they didn't want to be a bother but loved him and his movies so much…would he mind signing their napkins? He wrote quickly, they left, we left, and as we parted he said, "I wonder how far they will get before they realize I am not Montgomery Clift"?

Garth Brooks

Nobody in music has sold more records than Garth. He was hosting The Academy of Country Music Celebrity Golf Tournament. When my youngest daughter Christine, who was 17 at the time, found out, she asked if she could attend and meet him as she was and is a huge fan. Since she was up to par at

school, I allowed it. The night before the event, she asked me if it would be all right to write him a letter and give it to him. I told her it would be all right, so she wrote him a letter. In the letter she told him that she and her friend Scott had always played his CD and that the song "The River" had special meaning for them. Scott was tragically killed in an auto accident. The next morning, on the way to the event, she asked again if it was all right. So, when I introduced her and took her photo with him, she shyly presented the letter to him and we went to my golf cart. She asked, "Do you think he'll really read it, Dad?"

I looked at her pleading eyes and answered, "Of course. He is a class act. I don't know if he will have time today with all the doings but I am sure he will." After golf we went to the dinner and Garth had a plane to catch but grabbed his guitar (with no band) and before dinner said, "I am really sorry I have to leave early but I would love to sing two songs for you. The first one is one I haven't done in a while, but I want to do it tonight because…well, just because I want to."

He sang…"The River." With tears in our eyes, I looked at Christine and said, "Honey, he read your letter."

Jim Brown

Jim Brown is one of the greatest running backs in the history of the NFL, if not *the* greatest. I did two movies with Jim: *Ice Station Zebra* and a two-hour movie of the week, *Police Story*. Jim's role in *Zebra* was the first time an African American was playing a role where the script did not specify race. On the day we

met, he had gone to the dailies and I had some scenes in them as well. He has a great, dry sense of humor which I saw that day. He complimented me on my work and I complimented him on his football career and transition to movie star. He told me I must have been a great athlete as well and when I asked why he said, "All great athletes have big asses so you must have been great." We laughed.

Over the years Jim has given so much back to the community. He goes into the inner city and deals with the gangs trying to lead them into a productive direction. One night, The City of Hope was honoring George Foreman during his second reign as Heavyweight Champion of the World. In his remarks, he told a story about Jim. He said that when he was a young man, he was a bully and would do bad things and one day he saw Jim Brown on a television Public Service spot telling young people to do something positive with their lives — to go out and join the Job Corps. Big George did and was ever grateful to Jim Brown.

George Burns

George Burns one of the *all-time greats* in every phase of his beloved showbiz. I was fortunate enough to do a commercial with him where I had to do an impression of him… singing. At the audition, I saw some of the better impressionists there and so I figured I had better do something different, so I did his act. He had just performed at a major charity affair and had followed a very funny Freddie Prinze.

George's opening, and what I did for the audition, was "The boy is good *and* was funny, so instead of me being funny I have decided to sing a couple of songs for you. If you like them, I will do one or two more…and if you don't like them, I will do 40 or 50…all ballads." Needless to say, the audience roared.

All the time he was talking, he had a cigar and his cigar holder and said, "When I was younger I used to like to smoke and drink and do *other things* and even though I am now too old to do those *other things*…you will notice I am still very careful how I insert my cigar into its holder." Another roar.

When we were filming the commercial for Shower Massage, he regaled us all day with wonderful stories. He loved what he did and was so beloved. I never heard an unkind word said about Mr. Burns. I *had* heard a story about him and his best friend, Jack Benny, and asked him if it was true. He said it was, so I will relate it to you.

In the old days, performers working at The Palladium in London would sail across the ocean and arrive a week before they would perform. Manager Irving Fein handled both George and Gracie, and Jack and Mary (Livingston) Benny. Jack and Mary were headlining and George and Gracie were to follow. When they showed up at the hotel, Mary was in the lobby, met Gracie, and off they went when told that Jack was up in the suite. George picked up the house phone and called Jack. Jack told him the suite number and told him to come right up. When he hung up, Jack removed all his clothes except for his shoes, socks, garters, Homburg hat, attaché case and umbrella.

Knock. knock. knock…"Come in." Burns had sent the maid up.

President George H.W. Bush

I have been with President George Herbert Walker Bush a number of times alone as I emceed the Safari Club Convention where he was the guest speaker a couple of times, and he General **Schwarzkopf** and I, along with the Secret Service, would get a private tour of the convention displays before they would actually open.

These were certainly memorable events, but my favorite story about him has to do with my Kay. We were at a City of Hope dinner honoring him while he was in office and he was doing many private photo ops with sponsors, VIP's, and a small group of us were to be in the last photo. Kay noticed that the President's bow tie was askew and had been for *all* the prior pictures. As we walked in for the photo, without warning, Kay reached for the President's neck and said, "Mr. President, Barbara would never forgive me if I didn't straighten your tie." Kay was completely unaware of the attention she was getting from the Secret Service men. The president responded so graciously, "Oh, thank you so much and you're right. That's the first thing Barbara would have done as well." A very classy man.

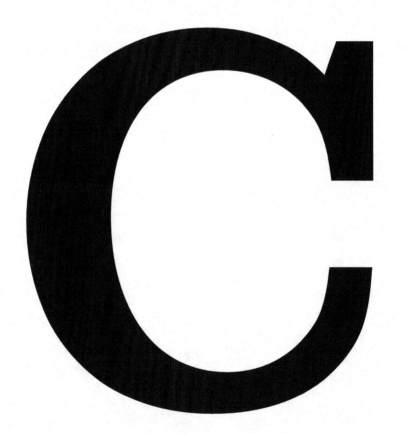

Roy Campanella

Three-time National League Most Valuable Player, who was confined to a wheelchair after a terrible automobile accident. His wife Roxie was an angel. I emceed a lot of their golf tournaments for them and was asked to emcee a dinner that would honor Roy. I kid you not, as Jack Paar used to say, this really happened. I am at the podium telling humorous stories when a man wearing coveralls and oblivious to everything going on, reaches up and lifts the podium and lowers it to the floor some two feet lower than the stage. The audience

roared with laughter as I just kept staring at this guy going about his business as if he was the only one in the room. As he started to leave, I called to him, "Hey, pal, what the hell are you doing?" And as if he came right out of a Three Stooges routine he said, "Just following instructions. They told me the speaker was in a wheelchair and I should put the podium and microphone on the floor." He turned and left and the loudest laugh was heard to come from, of course… Roy Campanella.

Chico Carrasquel

I may be the only Caucasian in history that had the nickname Chico. I was born and raised on the South Side of Chicago…you know, the part Bad, Bad Leroy Brown came from. I was the biggest White Sox fan in the world and being a shortstop, I idolized Alfonzo "Chico" Carrasquel. Chico was the slick fielding shortstop on the Sox and I wanted to be just like him, so I would have friends hit me ground ball after ground ball. This was baseball before the corporate baseball we know today. Players did not make big money, but boy, could they play the game, and Chico made history by becoming the first Latin player elected to the All-Star Game. I am so happy that Number 17 of the Chicago White Sox was a role model to look up to in the days before greed, disloyalty, cheating and steroids took over the game. Chico never made it to the Hall of Fame, but in my mind and my heart, he is there.

Wilt Chamberlain

Wilt the Stilt was the most dom-
inant center in the history of the
NBA and to this day, the only man
to score 100 points in a game. He
was a strong man and a terrific athlete, a great volleyball player and a
fine racquetball player. That's where
we met — at a racquetball club. He
was good and if he didn't agree with
your call, he could plant a shot right
in the middle of your back.

Well, one day, we were sitting
around discussing a book he wrote
that was coming to the stores. In the
book, Wilt claims to have bedded 25,000 women. My feeling on this was that
when he was reading the galley sheets, it was supposed to read 2,500. Okay. That,
I would have bought from him, but 25,000? So I called him on it.

"Wilt…25,000 women?!"

He looked at me and said, "Yes????"

To which I answered, "Wilt, that breaks down to a woman and a half a day,
every day, since you were 15 years old."

After a long, long pause he looked up and said, "*So?*"

As I got up, I turned to him and said, "You telling me a man of your fame
and stature that…No one came back for seconds?"

If he could have stopped laughing long enough to catch me he would have
probably killed me…

Governor John Connally

A figure in history as the other man shot when JFK was assassinated. I was
doing an event in San Antonio, Texas, when I was approached by a tall, distin-
guished-looking man. He asked if I would mind if he brought his wife over to

meet me. Needless to say, I went over to meet her. We sat and chatted for about an hour — what a fascinating experience. In that conversation, long before modern science proved him right, he pointed out that he was a lifelong hunter and the one thing a real hunter knows is where a bullet comes from. He told me that he never lost consciousness and there was no shot from the grassy knoll, but all three shots came from behind. To this day, when I remember him telling me that, the hair on the back of my neck stands up.

Bill Cosby

The "Coz." That wonderful rare breed of comedian who never found the need to work dirty. In concert, there has never been anyone funnier than Bill. He relates to all people of all faiths and colors and he relates to humanity. When *The Cosby Show* was number one in the world, that was every family. Period.

Long before that hit, though, Coz used to host a tennis tournament and he could really play...carried his own pro with him. Well, he would win his own tournament. One day I said to him, "Bill, you have some of the A players grumbling. You are not supposed to win your own event." He said, "Then let them practice a little more and grumble a little less."

After his great success, he was on hiatus from his show and shooting a movie at Universal, where I was shooting *Murder, She Wrote*. One day Richard Paul, who played Mayor Sam Booth on the show, and I were walking back to the set from lunch and heard, "No! No! There are no roles for any white guys named Mâsak...especially white sheriffs."

Richard said, "Holy smokes, that sounds like Bill Cosby." I said, "It is."

We turned the corner and there sitting on an apple box wearing a rumpled brown suit and smoking a cigar was television's biggest comedy star. After a few laughs Coz said, "Look at this guys: big, rich television star, can call my own shots, and I pick a movie where I don't even get to wear a nice wardrobe…just this one ugly suit for the whole movie." The movie was *Ghost Dad*, where, of course, he played a ghost.

He and his wife Camille have donated millions to colleges all over America and I will never forget his comment when some insensitive reporter put a microphone in his face after Bill's son, Ennis, was murdered and asked Bill how he felt. Bill graciously replied, "I have lost *my hero*." Bill remains one of mine.

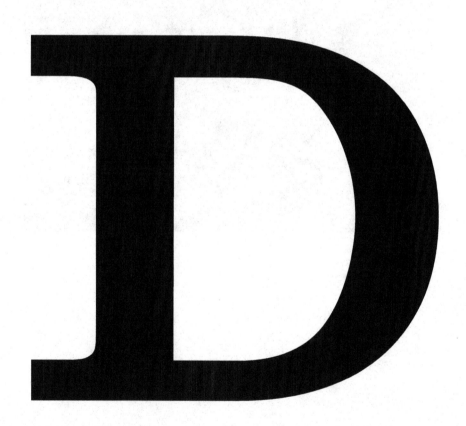

Sammy Davis Jr.

I never got to see the great Al Jolson perform live and he was always billed as The World's Greatest Entertainer. Well, in my lifetime, that title could also apply to Sammy. He could do it all: sing, dance, play instruments, and do impressions and comedy. He never failed to receive a standing ovation at the end of his performances.

I saw him many times before we actually met. He and Altovise opened their Beverly Hills home for a charity event. At this period in his life, Sammy was hosting his own talk show and I had some fifteen network commercials running. Someone at the door asked Sammy if he knew me. He replied, "Hell, man, this guy's on television more than I am and I've got my own show."

In the years after that I was with Sammy a few more times. The last time, right before he passed, was when he and Altovise came to a Dodger game and we were seated in the dugout seats (they no longer exist). When I saw him, I asked if Tommy [Lasorda] knew he was there. He didn't but Sammy said he didn't want to bother Tommy. I told him, "Tommy would never forgive me if I didn't let him know that you were here." Tommy, of course, came out to see him and pay his respects. Imagine, Sammy not wanting to bother anyone.

I did get to tell him that my act on the world touring Rolling Along show was called *A View of Vegas* and that the only thing I said in my own voice was, "Ladies and gentlemen, The Sands Hotel proudly presents Mr. Sammy Davis, Jr." My act was a tribute to him and consisted of impressions. He was a great mimic and actually had a hit record doing impressions. You learn from the best and he was.

Joe DiMaggio

The Yankee Clipper — the classiest major leaguer of them all. We were playing in a golf tournament for the legendary producer David Wolper when someone asked Joe if he got to know Babe Ruth. His reply, which to me spoke volumes of the man, was, "No, but I did dress right next to a man named Lou Gehrig."

Joe was a man of great mystery…always a classy dresser with suit and tie. He became known to a generation of new fans as Mr. Coffee, as he was their spokesman for years. The Dodgers were hosting The All-Star Game and The Legends Game in the same year, 1980. So many Hall of Fame players were coming to participate. Joe, Duke Snyder and Willie Mays were going to make their entrance from center field. Mickey Mantle had been invited but couldn't make it, but these three famed NY Center Fielders did and created a buzz. I was blessed in being allowed to work out and take batting practice with the Dodgers

and was allowed some hallowed access. I always made it a point to pick up a practice ball and put it in my pocket and then find some kid in the stands and give it to him or her. This was also an occasion for me as host of the LA portion of the Jerry Lewis MDA telethon to do a couple of on-camera interviews; old friend Ernie Banks agreed to do one as did the great Willie Mays.

Later on in the Hall of Fame locker room, I was in awe as I looked around: Joe D., Mays, Snyder, Pee Wee Reese, Henry Aaron, Banks, Sandy Kofax, Drysdale and more…my childhood flashed before me. One of Joe's best friends was there and saw the outline of the ball in my pocket and asked me if I wanted Joe to sign the ball. Remember, it was a practice ball from the field, but being no fool, I said, "Yes." Joe graciously signed the ball and as I started to put it back in my pocket, Willie Mays looked over and said, "Hey, Ron, I'm good enough for the interview, but you don't want me to sign the ball?" I was tongue-tied. He signed that ball, as did Erie, Lou Brock and Bob Feller. What a great ball…one I did *not* give to a kid that day.

The one thing I remember most about that day is that with a room full of Hall of Fame players…they *all* stopped what they were doing and turned to watch Joltin' Joe pull on those pinstripes.

It was magic.

Neil Armstrong and Joe DiMaggio.

General James Doolittle

The legendary General who led the bombing mission over Tokyo during World War II — a major turning point in history, for which he was awarded the Congressional Medal of Honor. He was being honored by The Silver Dollar Club at The Sportsman's Lodge in Studio City, CA; already around 80 years of age but full of energy.

I emceed the event. The wonderful Martha Raye was there to salute the General. Martha was an Honorary Colonel in The Green Berets and deservedly so. She entertained more troops in more foxholes and bunkers than anyone during the Vietnam conflict and had been entertaining the troops since World War II. She asked me if I could get the General up to say something, so I said, "General, would you be kind enough to jump up here on stage and say something?"

To a standing ovation and thunderous applause, he marched from the back of the room and literally without using his hands…jumped onto that stage. He turned to face the applauding crowd. When they finally stopped, he quietly said, "*Something*," and jumped off the stage to much laughter and applause. What a quiet hero.

Joe Higgins, General Doolittle, Me and Dodger catcher Steve Yeager.

Anne Meyers Drysdale

One of the greatest athletes ever, man or woman. Anne is the widow of the late Hall of Fame Dodger pitcher Don Drysdale and the first woman ever signed to an NBA contract. She is in basketball's Hall of Fame and is now doing broadcasts on television for basketball. Years ago, I used to bring 30 world-class athletes to Palm Springs or Arizona for a Super Bowl Weekend of fun and games. Annie was the only female among the group and that first year we were teammates… wow!! What a dynamo!

The company we did the event for would bring some 500 of their best achievers as a reward and to meet and become teammates with these world-class champions. But in every group there is *always* someone from the sandlot who thinks they are as good as or better than the pro. One such person continued to challenge Annie to play him one on one. She politely declined often, but finally the big mouth, trying to impress his friends, told them she was afraid to play him. That was the last straw. Annie not only beat him…she shut him out. He never scored and I am sure never heard the end of it from his friends.

Kay, Comedian Tom Dreeson, Me and Anne.

Stein Eriksen

In 1952, Stein Eriksen won the Olympic Gold Medal in the Giant Slalom by two seconds and put downhill skiing on the map. Los Angeles Dodger star first baseman Steve Garvey used to host a celebrity ski event held in Deer Valley, Utah to benefit the Special Olympics program. We would all stay at Stein's magnificent lodge. Before the celebrity races, Stein would gather some 50 or so Special Olympians, some who had never skied before, and he would give them a one-hour lesson. He would then take them to the top of the mountain…and without fear they would all ski down. I was so impressed with how he simplified the instructions to them. "Take it nice and easy and follow the person in front of you. When they turn, you turn; when they stop, you stop." He would place a few of us celebrities at various spots in the lone; one to lead, one a little further back, etc. Stein was the smoothest skier you can imagine. It was as though his feet and skis had been welded together. We would zigzag down the mountain as Stein offered encouragement to all. To me he would say, "Ron …put your legs together," and my answer was always, "They *are* Stein…but at the *top*." An incredible and giving man.

Peter Falk

One of the best actors on the planet, he is perhaps best known as the rumpled and seemingly confused Lieutenant Columbo. He received consecutive Oscar nominations for his supporting roles in *Murder, Inc.* (1960) and *Pocketful of Miracles* (1961).

One of the most giving actors I have ever had the pleasure of working with. I was so honored to be asked to guest star in a *Columbo* Movie of the Week. It was directed by long time friend and brilliant actor/director Patrick McGoohan. Patrick was one of the stars of my first film *Ice Station Zebra*.

One day Patrick was having lunch in the Universal Grill and caught my eye, so I went over to say hello. He was reading the *Columbo* script that he was to Guest Star in as well as direct. He looked at me and said "No, no, it is too small a role for you and you wouldn't do it…" He knew he had me, so I said "Patrick…for *you* I would do a walk on." He didn't know that I already knew Peter, so he walks me over to Peter's office, and Falk looks up and says "Hell, Ron don't have to read for me…he can play any part he wants, including mine." One of the really fun shoots in my career as Peter and Patrick are two of the most brilliant minds in our business. Peter had his right eye removed as well as a tumor when he was three years old and never let that stop him from pursuing his dreams.

George Foreman

Two stories immediately come to mind about this Gold Medal-winning Olympian and two-time Heavyweight Champion of the World. Kay and I were in ringside seats for his fight against champion Michael Moore. Big George was trying to win the title back at the age of 45; an impossible feat for any other man. George was holding his own but was taking some punishment as the younger Moore was getting some solid and heavy shots in on Big George, but George would take one step back and come in for more. Foreman did not sit down between rounds and you could see that Moore could not believe that this older man was still coming at him and not resting between rounds. Some wells were forming under George's eyes and I remember telling Kay that I really hope he doesn't get seriously hurt. This giant teddy bear looked over our way, smiled and winked. He went out in the 10th round and got Moore's attention with a short right hand and a short time later knocked him out with another one. 45-year-old George Foreman was once again the Heavyweight Champion of the World. When asked if it wasn't time to quit because of his age, George remarked, "I will when one of these younger fellas can knock me down." Oddly enough, they couldn't.

Clark Gable

The King. When I was doing Stanley Kowalski in a Chicago production of *A Streetcar Named Desire,* we had an integrated cast and Hecht, Hill and Lancaster had a nationwide talent search on to find an unknown African American for one of their films. The talent scout came backstage and talked to us all. He told me that obviously there could be nothing for me in the film they were casting, but if I ever came to California to look him up.

A year later, I did. He was a script supervisor and assistant to Burt Lancaster. They were almost finished with the filming of *Run Silent, Run Deep.* I was introduced to Burt, who was very kind to me, and as we were walking to the set had to pass Gable's dressing room. When asked if I would care to meet him, I said "Oh God, yes!!" When I was a kid, we went to the movies and the coming attractions always had words scrawling across the screen…you know: TERRIFYING…SHOCKING…that kind of thing; GABLE'S BACK and GARSON'S GOT HIM. Well, when we got to Gable's room, the door was open and he was sitting with his back to the open door. When Burt got Gable's attention, he looked over his shoulder at me and smiled and all I could see was the word ADVENTURE. What a gentleman. He welcomed me to Hollywood and wished me luck in my career. He will be forever emblazoned in my brain next to the word ADVENTURE.

Steve Garvey

Where do I begin with Steve? He is like my younger brother; he is my daughter Christine's godfather. He was the Golden Glove first baseman for the Los Angeles Dodgers. We first met in the early '70s when I was filming a pilot at the

stadium called *Hey Coach*. I was the coach of a group of youngsters who would
meet and get to ask questions of athletes. Steve, along with Dodgers Steve Yeager
and Davey Lopes, were the guest stars in the pilot. From that day on, both the
Steves and I became like brothers — Steve Yeager actually lived across the street
from us. They both hosted their own golf tournaments, which I would emcee

for them, and both played on the Josephina's basketball team with me. It was all
Dodgers and one actor…me.

Over the years Steve would host golf, tennis, ski, and deep-sea fishing tournaments and we would travel the world together: Ireland, Hawaii, Deer Valley,
Utah, Chicago, Las Vegas, San Diego and other parts of America. I could tell
you hundreds of stories about Steve, who, over the years, has been the subject of
both good and bad publicity, both of which I take with a grain of salt; praised
when he is up, maligned when he is down, but always the same calm demeanor.
You could never tell whether Steve went 0-4 or 4-4. I walked out of the stadium
hundreds of times with him and watched him sign every autograph for every
kid and grown-up. At this writing, Steve still holds the National League record
for consecutive games played. That's one of the stories I will tell.

The Dodgers were playing in the World Series and I picked Steve up at his home in Calabasas, California to drive him to the game. While he never misses a plane, he is not the most punctual person either. I'm on time or early; he's always a tad behind. Well, on this day, he was puttering around and signing pictures and gathering things and I am telling him that there will be a lot of traffic.

Finally, we are in the car.

We drove to the stadium. When we arrived, the cars in all lanes to the stadium were backed up. I started to get a little panicky; Steve continued to read the newspaper. I got a stadium cop's attention, called him to the car and told him that I had to get into the park. "Everyone does." I explained that I had to get in there *now* as I had the Dodger first baseman with me. I am sitting there thinking that tomorrow's headline was going to read: *Garvey's Consecutive Game Streak Halted By Actor.* The cop peeked in the window and saw Steve, sat on the hood of my car and directed me to drive on the sidewalk all the way from Sunset Boulevard to the pass gate where we entered, Steve still reading and smiling. I said to him, "How the hell can you sit there and smile? I was afraid the streak would end." He calmly said, "Ron, I might have missed batting practice but, I wouldn't have missed the game because eventually they would have had to open the gates to let the fans in." I could have killed him…but that would have really ended the streak.

Cary Grant

Cary Grant, *movie star.* He had it all: looks, talent and charm. We met at Drake Field at UCLA where we were all contributing our time and talent for the Special Olympics Program. This one area of the field was used for instant photos. A Special Olympian would sit between two celebrities, have their Polaroid photo taken and signed. I lucked out, for who was coming to take the other chair but Cary Grant. At that time I had a summer series on television called *Love Thy Neighbor* and it was a hit. When he introduced himself, he said, "Hello, Ron. I'm Cary Grant and my daughter Jennifer loves your show." I felt like I had a mouthful of marbles when I tried to say thank you. He added, "I don't know if anyone here will know me. They are so young and I haven't made a movie in years." I told him not to worry, that he was Cary Grant and his movies were shown on television all the time.

As the first youngster approached with his nametag, I said, "Hi ya, Joey, I'm Ron Masak and this is Cary Grant." The youngster's eyes lit up and a huge smile greeted Mr. Grant and the boy said, "Cary Grant, I love you." Needless to say, he had not been forgotten.

He was a frequent visitor to Dodger Stadium and was often up in the O'Malley box with the likes of Danny Kaye or Frank Sinatra. One night Frank

brought him down to Lasorda's office before a game and Tommy always graciously would send for the new players who had never met these giants. Well, on
this night, he had Pedro Guerrero go get newcomer Mariano Duncan, a player
from the Dominican. Mariano came into Tommy's office with a photographer
and, not recognizing Sinatra, gently nudged Frank out of the way, put his arm
around Cary and said, "I take picture with *you*." Sinatra laughed the loudest.

Each year at Dodger Stadium heroes from the LAPD are honored on the
field with the Valor Awards. Year after year, Gregory Peck would announce these
awards and read the actual account of the heroic effort of each officer. One year,
Mr. Peck could not attend and they asked Cary Grant to do it. As he stood next
to me in the dugout seats going over the script, he pointed out that he wasn't
sure he could do justice to these heroic men and women. Finally, on the field
there was Cary Grant doing the *perfect* impression of Cary Grant reading, bob-
bing and weaving and just oozing charm. When he finished, he came to the
seats, looked at us and meaningfully asked if he was okay. "Okay?…Why you
were…Cary Grant."

H

Susan Hayward

Academy Award Winner. This marvelous actress was going to be doing her first television experience: A project called *Heat of Anger*. She was replacing Barbara Stanwyck who had become ill. I was in the first shot being done. It was her, Lee J. Cobb and me. I was a detective. It was a hot day and we were filming on location at a construction site. As she came on the set, I introduced myself and told her who I was and what I was playing and how I had been in love with her

all my life. She smiled and told me, "I was nervous all morning as this is my first television. You'll never know how much those words just helped me to relax." With that, she hiked up her skirt, straightened her hose and said, "OK, folks, let's roll some film." She got on a construction elevator and rode it up. What a pro.

Katharine Hepburn

While we were filming a scene in *Ice Station Zebra* where I fall through the ice, we got a call that Katharine Hepburn was on the lot and was coming over to see her old friend John Sturges who had directed Spencer Tracy in *Bad Day at Black Rock*. Sturges, knowing the scene he was to shoot, had already released Ernie Borgnine for the day as well as Patrick McGoohan, so it was to be Rock and me and a couple of stuntmen. When I was told Miss Hepburn and her niece Katharine Houghton were on their way, I started to excuse myself to go elsewhere but Rock insisted I stay. When she got to the dressing room, Rock jumped up so fast I thought he hit his head on the ceiling. He graciously introduced me to this legend, they chatted, and she said kind things to me and wished me a long career and told us both how much Spence loved this studio (MGM). When she left, Rock asked me how I felt. I told him deeply honored. He told me that his heart was pounding twice as fast as normal. See, folks, even the biggest of movie stars can still be…a fan.

Joe E. Tata, Me, Chuck, Kay, and Christine.

Charlton Heston

Chuck is another of those actors who is a real movie star. He used to host his own celebrity shoot for charity. He probably knows the Constitution as well as anyone in history did and I often wondered if he might not have been President of the United States had he chose to run.

We were at a black-tie dinner honoring President Bush (the first) and it turns out Chuck was to be one of the speakers. When introduced, he came out in sports jacket, slacks and an open shirt, no tie, and delivered one of the most articulate speeches I have ever heard. He read the preamble to the Constitution and touched on certain amendments. When he finished, he turned to the President and said, "Mr. President, while I would be honored to stay and have dinner with you, I promised my grandson that I would be having dinner with him this evening and a promise is a promise." He left to a standing ovation. Quite a man.

Bob Hope

Probably the most successful all-around talent in history: Vaudeville star, Broadway star, radio star, recording star, movie star, television star, live performer... incredible talent. I was with this legend a few times in my life and was asked to emcee a Vietnam Veteran's dinner honoring Robert Mitchum and Mr. Hope. I was so honored.

But my favorite time with him was in Florida at the Payne Stewart golf tournament benefiting the Florida Hospital for Cancer research. Bob was there filming his special for NBC and was riding around the course with Payne and playing a hole here and there with certain groups. When they got to us, they stayed and played our last three holes with us and I had some of his sponsors in my group. On the last hole, Mr. Hope was about 185 yards out and kept asking Payne, "What do you think, Payne, 184 –185? Huh? What do you think?" Payne agreed to the distance. Bob again said, "Yes, that's what I think, 184-185." He sang on his back swing and hit his ball about 150 yards. He looked at Payne and said, "Yes sir, I was right; it was 184-185." We all laughed.

When we all had pitched to the green, I noticed one of the sponsors, who was in total awe that he was playing golf with Bob Hope and Payne Stewart. He was standing over his putt of about eight feet and I said to him, "If you make this putt, it may be on the Bob Hope Special." He smiled and stood over his put and I continued, "And if you *miss it*...you will *definitely* be on it." He froze. He could not take the putter back and in front of a large crowd around the 18th Green. Bob rattled off a few lines at the poor man's expense, took the putter out of his hands and said, "He's one of my sponsors, folks...that's a *gimme*."

Rogers Hornsby

The last right-handed hitter to bat over 400, this Hall of Famer was a major league scout. One summer I was playing baseball on a team called The Evening Stars at McKinley Park in Chicago. I was two weeks away from my 16th birthday and playing in a league for 18-year-olds and over. We played double-headers all week and I was on a roll, hitting for power and average and though I never had great speed I had deceptive speed and was stealing bases  on a delayed steal, when the catcher was throwing the ball back to the pitcher and the infielders would relax. I was fielding my shortstop position pretty well, too. This grey-haired gentleman wearing a uniform with *Rajah* (I would later find out that was his nickname) on his chest talked with my coach and wanted to offer me a contract to play in the White Sox (my team) Organization. He took me home and met with my mom, telling her of the offer of $8,500 to sign. That would have been like a million to us. She explained to him that she would really like to see me finish high school first. He thought I was 18 and out of there. She told him my real age, but the offer stood. She looked at me and told me that as an athlete, at the age of 30 I would be on the way out, but that as an entertainer I would still be learning my craft…and could always play ball. I guess Mom knew best. I didn't play for the White Sox…but in my heart I know that I could have. And to be offered a contract by the great Rogers Hornsby — a memory I treasure.

Rock Hudson

Movie star: I did my first movie with Rock, *Ice Station Zebra*. I worked 4½ months on that film and found him to be as nice a human being as I had ever met. Obviously, in later years, his untimely death brought much-needed attention to the AIDS crisis.

On the first day of filming, he was kind enough to come over and introduce himself as if he needed to do that; like we didn't know who he was. He was a tall 6'4" handsome man with a great sense of humor and told wonderful stories and played wonderful practical jokes. Seven of us who were going to be on the film regularly would play Gin or Hearts between set ups in his trailer and he loved fudge. My Kay is a great cook and baker so she would make cookies, cake, brownies, and fudge and we would take them to the set or his trailer and eat them while we played. One day while enjoying fudge, Rock told me to get Kay on the phone. I called and he got on the phone and said to my young wife, after thanking her for all the goodies, "… And, Kay, most of all, thank you…for *just being you*," and hung up. I looked at him as did all the other guys there and I said, "Well, you SOB. How the hell am I ever going to have any romance with my wife after Rock Hudson says *that* to her?"

Now at this point I have to tell you that Patrick McGoohan and his wife and Kay and I had gone to dinner a couple of nights before and Patrick sent Kay a dozen long-stem roses. So now Rock says that to Kay. That night as we sat down to dinner, the doorbell rings. I answer it and it is a florist. Now Kay is looking at me like she is thinking, "Isn't that sweet, my husband was jealous of Patrick's flowers," and before she could say a word I said, "Don't look at me. I didn't send them." Four dozen baby tea roses and baby's breath, and a card that read,

"Dear Kay…*You know*…Rock." That was 1967 and she still has those flowers and that card in a frame. Needless to say, I went looking for him the next day.

Lloyd Haynes, who later went on to star in *Room 222,* was one of our cardplaying group and was a balladeer. When Rock found that out, he asked Lloyd to get his guitar and play something. Rock told him to take his car and go get it as Lloyd's car was in the parking lot outside the front gate. As he left, Rock thought of a prank so he got on the phone and called the guard at the front gate, Ken Hollywood (that was his real name), and told him to stop Lloyd and tell him that he (Rock) had reported his car stolen. Kenny informed Rock that it was too late as Lloyd had just passed, so quickly Rock told Kenny to tell Lloyd that they needed Rock on set so he was just to put the car keys back in Rock's street clothes pocket in the closet. When Lloyd got back and was doing so, Rock had a guard look in and say, "Hey, you. What are you doing with your hand in that man's pocket?" I thought Lloyd was going to wet his pants until he heard us all laughing outside.

I would never assume that a star of that stature could remember everyone he has ever worked with, so every time I would see Rock at a dinner or social function I would remind him of my name and he would always say, "I know, I know."

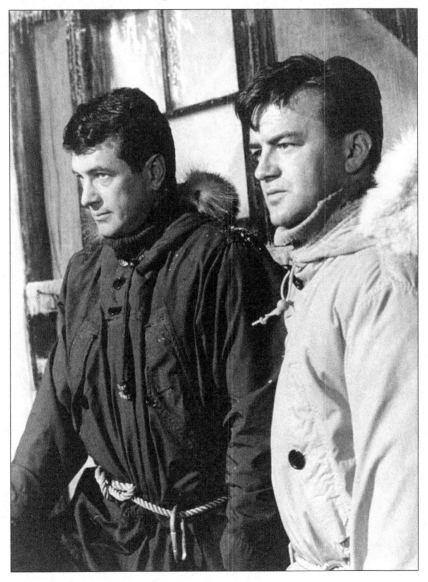

Rock and Me in Ice Station Zebra.

Well, years later, I was filming a *Quincy* at Universal Studios and I was standing by the corner store when I heard, "Ron Mâsak, you son of a bitch...Do you believe I remember you *now?*" I looked up and a good ¾ of a block away was this handsome man with a mustache and smoking jacket. It was Rock laughing all the way up to me. He was shooting the pilot for *McMillan and Wife*. I got even, though. I guest-starred on the show and got to arrest the tallest pink bunny in history. You will never hear anyone whoever worked with him, cast or crew, say anything bad or negative about him. He was one of the nice ones.

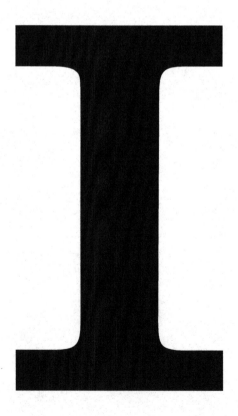

Julius (Dr. J) Irving

One of the NBA's all-time greats and one of the first to fly from the top of the key to slam-dunk a basketball. Look up his ABA and NBA statistics; they will astound you. Dr. J and I met at a couple of charity events, but got to know each other when we did Tom Kite's golf video together. This is one of the classiest men around. Because of the influence of his mother, he learned quickly that it was more important to be a good person than it was to be a great basketball player. He is a writer and loves poetry, and, even more importantly, he loves people.

He had just retired from basketball and was taking up golf when we were doing the video and was already down to a 12 handicap — a super athlete and a super friend. We see each other occasionally in Chicago where we both participate in Steadman Graham's Athletes Against Drugs program.

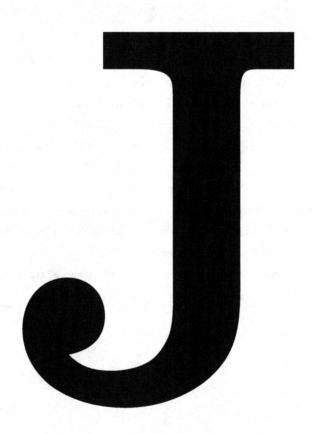

Kareem Abdul-Jabbar

Scored the most points in the history of the NBA. Kareem loved to play in the annual Hollywood Stars game at Dodger Stadium and is one of LA's most beloved athletes. Kareem, of course, always played first base and got the longest and loudest ovation. It made no difference how big a movie star was playing: Kevin Costner, Tom Selleck, Billy Crystal — none got anywhere near what Kareem got. I was fortunate enough to play for 33 straight years and I would only have three prayers to God before each game. They were: "Please, God, this is not how I earn my living so please don't let me get hurt; Please, God, don't let me strike out in front of Lasorda as I will never hear the end of it, and, most important, God, *please* don't let them introduce me immediately after Kareem."

We actually filmed a musical commercial together for Nestle's Crunch. I was a dancing, moving traffic cop in downtown LA, with real traffic and at the end, Kareem's limo pulls up and he pops up through the top and takes a bite, saying, "And that's why I like Nestlé's Crunch." Well, for whatever reason, he couldn't get the

The Hollywood Stars First Baseman.

bite on the exact cue and if he did, something technical would happen like some of the bar falling down his front. To offer a little levity I said, "Sure, look at this. The guy puts a round ball through a round hoop more than anyone in the history of the game with tons of flesh leaning all over him, and he can't get a little candy bar in his mouth." We got the spot done and it was an award winner.

Bruce Jenner

Decathlon Champion; still owes me $12 (golf). He is a great athlete, always working to improve his game. He, Garvey and I were playing in Ireland and we each had caddies that had been there forever. We teed off and after Bruce hit his second shot he dropped another ball to see if he could correct what he did and Seamus, my caddie, said, "What's he doing?" I tried to explain. I told him in my country they call it a Mulligan. I asked what they'd call it over here and he said, "We call it…he's hitting 4."

Sorry, Bruce…had you paid me the $12, I wouldn't have told this story.

Pope John Paul II

The holiest of holy men. The first time we were in his presence, Kay was pregnant with our youngest daughter. I was filming *The Neighborhood* in New York and Kay came to visit me. It was Pope John Paul's first visit to New York as the Pope. He was going to offer Mass at St. Patrick's Cathedral, which was only a brisk walk from our hotel. I was to have the weekend off from filming. It was dark and raining and they had blocked all entrances to Manhattan, but Kay really wanted to go. I tried to explain the odds of us ever getting close enough to see him, but she wanted to go and go we did in a heavy downpour. Well, it had to be my saintly wife because we were right there at the foot of the cathedral stairs. We listened to the Mass and when it ended, as God is my judge, the doors opened and it stopped raining immediately as the Pope stepped out into

the sunshine and blessed all who were there. We stayed a few minutes and went back inside and it started raining again. I looked at Kay and guess what? She didn't get to see him; when he came out, there a pickpocket in the crowd trying to steal something and Kay yelled at him to get out of there.

So, back to the hotel we go and a disappointed lady on my hands. She knew he was going to be there again the next day and wanted to go back. I tried to discourage her this time by pointing out how lucky we were to get that close once. Guess what? I woke up the next morning and she was gone…still dark and raining and my wife in New York, alone and pregnant. She left a note that she was going back to see the Pope. I panicked and dressed and wondered what the odds were on finding her. I ran as fast as I could go and, believe it or not, I found her in the same spot we were in the day before. Now, to me, *that* was a miracle…as well as what happened next. The doors opened, the rain stopped, the Pope blessed us all and Kay saw it this time. He went back in and we all just stayed there having been in his presence. After a while, a second-floor window opened and he appeared, blessed us again and spoke in English telling us to go home now as he was going to eat something.

Kay got to see him several times after that: Downtown LA, Dodger Stadium and Rome. Now if you ever see me or Kay, have us tell you about her trip to Rome and the Polish teacakes she baked for His Holiness…

K

Boris Karloff

King of the horror genre; the man who made Frankenstein's monster more human. Our theatre group went backstage to meet him and Julie Harris, who were starring in

The Lark, the story of the trial of Joan of Arc. Mr. Karloff was playing a bishop and was nominated for a Tony for his performance. We were backstage talking with Julie when in the shadows we saw this figure moving across the stage. One of the girls actually let out a little shriek.

We were always taught in our class to do research on the actors we were going to meet so we wouldn't ask a stupid question of them. Mr. Karloff was, actually, a dashing, sophisticated-looking man and my non-stupid question was, "Mr. Karloff, after all the years in the horror genre, how rewarding is it to have the public see you as this kindly Bishop?" His response was, and we loved it, "You know I only played the monster three times; in *Frankenstein, Bride of Frankenstein* and *Son of Frankenstein.* The monster wasn't *really* a bad man the way I played him. After all, it wasn't his fault that he got…the wrong brain."

Danny Kaye

One of the truly great all-around talents in show business. The first time I saw him was in Chicago at the Chicago Theatre. In those days, when a star was opening a film, they would do Vaudeville shows between the movies, and he could certainly control an audience. He stood behind the microphone and quietly started singing "Tiptoe through the Tulips" and by the time he had finished the song he had raced from the stage and ran up and down every aisle of the theatre's orchestra level singing and got back in just enough time to quietly finish the song.

The first time I met him was at Dodger Stadium. He was a huge Dodger fan and was a part owner of the Seattle Mariners, but he loved the Dodgers. He would come and sit in the O'Malley Booth, dressed in his soft fedora-type Dodger hat, his kerchief around his neck, a sweater jacket on and handmade soft shoes. Danny was a pilot, a gourmet Chinese cook and knew as much about med-

icine as many doctors. I saw this firsthand as Dodger shortstop Dave Anderson was suffering from back spasms and Danny had him lay on the floor, raise one leg and showed him an exercise that worked. He always lit up the room when he entered it. What a talented human being and a great leader in UNICEF. He lived life to its fullest…and shared that life with the world.

Grace Kelly

Her Royal Highness Princess Grace of Monaco was visiting MGM one day while we were filming *Ice Station Zebra* and since we were one of only two major films shooting on the lot at that time, the other being *The Legend of Lylah Clare*, Rock was the studio's selected ambassador to have lunch with the Princess and her party. She was an incredibly beautiful woman. Up until this day Rock always enjoyed joining the rest of the working cast for lunch in the commissary, sharing jokes and pranks. But on this day he had to excuse himself from us and be on his good behavior.

He had to behave, but *we* didn't have to. Rock was never fond of raisins, said they reminded him of boogers, so we would send him a bowl of raisin bran, a bowl of just raisins, rice pudding with raisins, etc. and every time we did, he would crack up. As we finished and were ready to go back to work he kindly called us over to meet her. This beautiful, gracious lady took the time to thank us all for the wonderful…raisins. I started to apologize and she told me it was not needed as she enjoyed a good joke as well as the next person. He *told* her the booger story…what a guy.

Ethel Kennedy

A spirited woman and a terrific athlete. One year I was doing the field announc-
ing for the Special Olympics and Ethyl was the representative of the family that
year (they all took turns). This was a wonderfully competitive field so we all came
up with the idea to have a final relay race; the celebrities against the Red Cross,
the volunteers, and the athletes. This wonderful lady, kicked off her shoes, hiked
up her skirt and was the fastest one on the track. We continued that Love In by
having everyone present in the stands join us on the field and we all held hands
and formed a circle of love around the track — a practice that they still use today.
It is a great program. I know…my nephew Donnie is a Special Olympian.

Larry King

One of television/radio's real icons. I first met him in Lasorda's office when he came to a game. The next time was when Tommy asked me to pick Larry up at the Century Plaza Hotel and drive him to Paul's Kitchen, Tommy's favorite Chinese restaurant. I drove down to pick up Larry in a convertible and proceeded to drive toward where I thought the restaurant was. It is on San Pedro in LA. On the freeway I suddenly saw a sign that said "San Pedro" and mistakenly got on it. I saw a

quizzical look on Larry's face, like, "Is this guy kidnapping me?" He remarked that he didn't think the restaurant was in the town of San Pedro, so, embarrassed, I turned around and headed for LA. I explained to him that while the food was magnificent the restaurant was in a very tough neighborhood. New Yorker Larry had no problems with that. As we approached the restaurant, I told him that we *had* to park inside the fenced area and not on the street. When we got there the only open slot at the time was for handicapped parking. As I pulled into it, I looked at Larry and told him to limp. We went in (I did move the car within minutes) and met Tommy, Whitey Herzog and the great Hollywood columnist James Bacon.

When we got in there and chatted a bit, Larry picked up a menu and started to order something small. Tommy grabbed the menu and told Larry, "No menus here" and for the next 90 minutes food never stopped coming. And, for one of the rare times in my life, I shut up and listened to some of the great stories about the news world, the baseball world and Hollywood. I spent quality time with four of the most charitable and generous men in the celebrity world.

Tom Kite

Great golfer and winner of the U.S. Open. We did a golf video together called *Tom Kite Playing Around With His Friends,* which were Julius (Dr. J) Irving, Claude Akins, and me. We spent a week at the Ventana Resort in Arizona filming and having a wonderful time. Tom and I played together in the Pro-Am at The Nissan Open at the Riviera Country Club in LA. It is now considered one of the best golf training videos ever made and we ad-libbed it all. He is a warm and wonderful quiet Texan.

We were standing on the practice range one morning and about three stalls away is one of those types that nothing goes right and nothing is ever his fault — blames the club, the traffic, his family, but never himself. After almost every shot he would mutter louder and louder and get angrier and angrier, slamming his clubs in his bag.

Tom took as much as he could. He walked quietly over to the man and introduced himself. The angry man was impressed. Tom asked if he could offer some advice. The man said, "Sure," so Tom said, "Sir, you don't now nor will you ever play golf that well to get that angry," and turned and walked back to us. The man picked up his bag and disappeared. Fore!!!

Sandy Koufax

The youngest man ever inducted into baseball's Hall of Fame. Arthritis cut short an incredible career, so I will just tell a short one about him. He is an incredibly shy man and when we were doing the Special Olympics he asked if we could kind of stay together. I was flattered that he would want to hang with me, then he explained why. He knew I could do enough talking for the both of us.

Someday someone may be as good, but no one will ever be a better pitcher than Sandy Koufax.

Angela Lansbury

The Rolls-Royce of our business, show business. Angela Lansbury has been a *star* for over 60 years and I was so honored to play Sheriff Mort Metzger to her Jessica Fletcher for eight of her 12 seasons on *Murder, She Wrote*. She is another one of those gracious ladies who always believed in *family first*. She is the most Emmy-nominated prime-time actress in history, a four-time Tony Award winner, 3-time Academy Award nominee, and the list goes on and on. I actually guest-starred twice on the show before becoming the sheriff. She always graciously welcomed all of her guest cast each week and made them feel comfortable. She set the tone of the work process and the whole company felt very classy.

I could tell you so many stories about this wonderful woman. She took this character created by the brilliant Peter Fischer and made her a worldwide regular visitor into homes all over the world. The list of guest stars on the show reads like the Who's Who of movies and television. Howard Hughes' widow, Jean Peters, actually came out of retirement to do the show. All the great MGM stars, like Van Johnson, Mickey Rooney, June Allyson, asked to do the show, and Peter Fischer and his staff wrote brilliantly for them. Stars that shone brightly on Broadway came to do the show and it opened new career doors for them. Good friend Jerry Orbach appeared on Broadway more than any actor in history and yet it was his work as Harry McGraw, opposite Jessica Fletcher, that led to *Law & Order* and major stardom.

Always reaching out to others, she found out that Madlyn Rhue had multiple sclerosis and was confined to a wheelchair; about to lose her medical insurance. Madlyn had done the show in 1989. Angela and Peter Fischer brought back Madlyn's character and when she did a show a year after that, Angela rented a motor home that was equipped for a wheelchair. Now *that's* class.

Five of my six children worked on the show as well as my son-in-law, Jimi Defilippis. My daughter Kathy played my only female deputy in one show and had a great line. My regular deputy said to her, "Make sure you get these reports right, because if you don't, the sheriff can be a bear." Her answer? "I know. He reminds me of my dad."

I know now how Ed McMahon felt all those years when asked what Johnny Carson was like, for not a day goes by where someone doesn't ask me what

Angela Lansbury is really like. I tell them that she can do it all: act, sing, dance. I never saw her late, angry, not prepared, or rude…never. I was asked, along with Bea Arthur, to introduce Angela to the audience when she was being inducted into Television Hall of Fame. I said then what I say now, "The Rolls-Royce of our business."

William Windom, Angela and The Sheriff.

Tommy Lasorda

Baseball's ambassador to the world. I thought Vince Lombardi hated to lose, but I have never seen anyone take a loss as hard as Tommy Lasorda. In baseball, the worst team will still win 1/3 of its games and the best team will lose 1/3 of its games. But as one who spent about a thousand nights in Tommy's office before and after a game I can tell you, he took every loss personally.

I got to know Tommy when he came up to the big club as the third-base coach. He brought energy and fire with him and a great outgoing spirit; he always said he bled Dodger Blue. Actor Jed Allan and I have been season ticket holders since we did *Ice Station Zebra* together. We always would chat with Tommy from our seats, and got to know him better when we would play in the Hollywood Stars game.

When he became manager, he invited us to come down to his office anytime. His office was special. One whole wall facing his desk was the Sinatra wall… only pictures of his pal, Francis Albert. On the side wall was the Rickles wall for Don Rickles, who would visit Tommy and tear into everyone. The other two walls were filled with the greatest players in the game, presidents of the United States and all his celebrity friends. Tommy had them, and they *all* came. One day he asked me why we only came down after a win and never after a loss. I explained that I was a happy-go-lucky guy and didn't want him or his players to think that I didn't care about the loss.

"Nonsense," he said. "Anyone can come down after a win but a *real* friend comes after a loss…so win or lose, you come on down." That night, they lost a really close game in the ninth inning. Jed looked at me and said, "I'm not going down." I looked back and said, "Didn't you hear him? Win or lose, he wants to see us." It took some convincing but he came with me and as I peeked around his office door a chair flew by my face and hit the Sinatra wall, knocking a dozen or so pictures off. I peeked back in and said, "Good night, Tommy." He came after us and suggested in the future, after a really tough one, to give him five minutes.

I could truly fill a book with stories on Tommy and our times together. I saw him do so many charitable things for the disabled and the underprivileged. I can't tell you how many times I saw him pick up his phone and call some kid who had written him a letter, or track down a youngster who had written him from a hospital…he answered them all. He even raised funds for a group of nuns who were being evicted. He allowed me to work out with his team for over 20 years…how blessed was I?

I was allowed on the field, in his office and watched a lot of baseball history close up. In Game One of the World Series against Oakland, it was the bottom of the ninth with two outs and a man on first. Former Dodger catcher and World Series co-MVP Steve Yeager and I were standing against the wall of the dugout seats when Dave Anderson walked to the on-deck circle, and the fans in the dugout got on Yeager. "What's Lasorda doing, Yeag…sending Anderson against the premiere reliever in the game?" Yeager just looked at the guy and said, "He's just in the circle Kirk Gibson is going to bat." The guy told Yeager that he was crazy; why Gibson is so hurt he's not even *in* the dugout. (Gibson had two bad legs and could hardly walk.) Yeager said, "Watch." And just then, Gibson comes into the dugout and onto the field and I go into a Howard Cosell impression: "Here he comes, folks, Willis Reed dragging his leg onto the court to face the Lakers for the Championship."

The rest is history, as the mighty Casey did *not* strike out that night but hit the most unbelievable home run in baseball history. Gibson limped around the bases pumping his arms. What a moment. Yeager and I went to Lasorda's office and it was hot and at least a hundred reporters were crammed in there. After a short while, Gibson peeked around the door wearing only a towel and yelled at the reporters, "What the hell you talking to him for? He didn't do anything. And, Tommy, I am really pissed at you." Now Gibson played baseball as though it was football; all-out hard. He looked like that drawing on the back of all the magazines that said "Draw me" - two-day stubble of beard and a menacing look. Tommy quiets the crowd and asks Kirk why he was mad.

"You never let me finish what I was saying to you. Remember when I came up to you and said, 'Tommy, I can pinch hit for you?'"

Tommy said, "Yes. That's why I sent you up there."

Kirk said, "But you didn't let me finish." A silent room all stared at Kirk. "Tommy, I can pinch hit for you...I *think*." A roar went up and Gibson disappeared. Just as Tommy was ready to start again, Gibson peeked around the door and said, "Hey, Sorda. I love you, man."

Jerry Lewis

One of my great heroes as a kid. He and Dean never failed to entertain. They made me laugh and made me feel good. He is considered a genius in France and not quite as appreciated as much in the US. Jerry holds every union card needed in the film business so he never had to wait. He could do it all; move furniture, set a light, run the camera, act, edit, direct, write. He was the first to use what is now a common practice, a video camera attached to a film camera so he could immediately review a scene, as he was in most of them.

I was the Los Angeles host for the MDA telethon for some ten years, and I was always amazed at the people who had so much hatred or jealousy that they would try to find fault with what he was doing as the national host. They would even call to see if he kept a lot of the money he raised. They never could see the good he was doing by raising millions of dollars for a cause that would have been *unnoticed* if it weren't for Jerry Lewis. He doesn't just do it one day a year, but works year round meeting all those corporations who back his concern, giving speeches and just doing good. I saw where that research money goes and if you ever drive by the UCLA Medical Center take a look at The Jerry Lewis Neuromuscular Center. I am quite proud of that building because I turned the first shovel of dirt for it, and all that from one of the world's great funny men. Bless him.

Vince Lombardi

Arguably the greatest football coach ever. He won three consecutive championships in a row; the last of the NFL Championships and the first two Super Bowls. I was lucky enough to be asked to star with him in the most successful non-theatrical film ever made, *Second Effort*. It is in the *Guinness Book of World Records* as such. More than 100 million people have seen it.

I will never forget the day I arrived to film and was driven to Lambeau field, home of the Green Bay Packers. They were changing the name of the street in front of it to Lombardi Avenue. Was I nervous? Not really, but I sure had a great respect for the man.

The next ten days gave me one of the great memories of my life. We did this wonderful film written by David Hayes, for whom I had done many shows in Chicago, so he wrote the character of Ron for me, which brings me to one highlight. Coach Lombardi kept calling *me* coach between shots and I assumed it was because he didn't remember my name so I kidded him by telling him that my name was the same as it was in the script. He said, "I know that, but in my business I am the coach and my responsibility is to guide my team to excellence. In your business *I* am the rookie and you are *my* coach." I was so honored and still am to this day.

He was a remarkable man who went to Mass every day and I have no doubts that if he chose the priesthood that he once considered, he would have been the first American pope. Jerry Kramer, the Hall of Fame right guard of the Packers, was also in the film. He told me that I got to know the coach more in ten days than Jerry did in ten years, as I got to socialize with him and the team didn't. He was a great motivator of men and one of his sayings was "Operate on Lombardi time," which meant if you were 10 minutes early, you were five minutes late, and he lived by that.

In the middle of the shoot, he invited me to join him at his club for dinner. I accepted. He asked if he should invite anyone else. I suggested the producer. Vince wanted to know if the producer had a suit. I told him that indeed he did back at the hotel. Vince told me to invite the producer and that we would leave at 6:00. At 5:46 p.m., Lombardi said, "Get in the car — he's late." I stalled as long as I could, saying that I had to run back to get my script. At 5:55, I was in the car and we started to pull away when producer Dean DiBrito pulled up next to us, jumped out of his car and into the coach's and was greeted with, "Don't be late again or we'll leave you." Dean sank in his seat like a little boy told to stand in the corner.

Every year at Super Bowl time you see a clip of The Coach on television walking to the front of the locker room and talking about football being a Spartan

game. That clip is from *Second Effort*. The only ad-lib he added to the film was in
that scene. I had just asked him what he would say to me if I was rookie in the
clubhouse. When he got to the front of the room, before he went to the written
dialogue, he looked at me and said, "My name is Vince Lombardi." WOW —
like he would ever have to tell anyone that.

Jerry became a friend in those ten days and asked if I would like to hear Lombardi's last locker room speech to the Packers from half time in Super Bowl II.
Jerry was also retiring that year and was writing a best-selling book called *Instant*

Replay, a title that came from the use of instant replay on television of his famous block in the famous Ice Bowl against the Dallas Cowboys that allowed Bart Starr to score the winning touchdown with just seconds on the clock. As Jerry began writing it, he got into the habit of carrying a tape recorder to the locker room. He was always the first to arrive; last to leave. As we got ready to listen, Jerry told me not to look for Knute Rockne or Pat O'Brien as that wasn't Lombardi's style, so we settled in and listened. Hall of Famer Willie Davis was talking to the team, letting them know that they weren't executing and needed to work harder in the second half and all of a sudden he says, "Quiet! Here's the old man."

Lombardi is heard to enter the room and says something like, "Gentlemen, if you go out and lose this game this afternoon, nobody will care or feel sorry for you, because you won it last year. But if you go out and win this game, you will do something that has never been done in the history of the NFL and that is win three consecutive World Championships...Our Father who art in heaven..." and he recited The Lord's Prayer. The locker room exploded with the players saying, "Let's go kick some ass," and they did. They dominated the second half. He did know how to motivate. At the end of the film, Lombardi gives me a football and tells me to get out there and make that sale. Some 40 years later, I still have that football.

Nancy Lopez

Hall of Fame golfer; Hall of Fame lady; all class. The first time I met Nancy I was with the legendary Jim Murray (Pulitzer Prize-winning writer who is also in baseball's Hall of Fame). Jim asked me to emcee an LPGA dinner and announce the next day. Nancy was just a rookie on the tour, but was winning everything in sight. She was humble and shy but brilliant on the course. She is a wonderful example of a wonderful upbringing. The more I talked with her the more impressed I was. I remember that on the first tee the next day, her dad was in her Pro-Am group. When it was time to introduce him, I mentioned what wonderful parents he and his wife must be to raise such a wonderful young lady. She never forgot that and over the years, when I would see her, she never failed to mention the kind words.

To fast forward her career, when she decided to retire from the tour in 2002, I was in her Pro-Am group at the Jamie Farr LPGA tournament in Toledo, Ohio, and got to play in her final event there. At the time, her husband, Ray Knight, was managing the Cincinnati Reds baseball team. The night before the Pro-Am was the Reds' family night at the stadium. She attended the luncheon, then she

and her children caught a flight to Cincinnati, attended the game, and flew back just in time for the Pro-Am. Family first.

Jamie had asked me to emcee the big gala and I was to introduce Nancy to 4,000 people. From the stage I looked down at this classy lady sitting there with her children. It was Jamie's tournament and the LPGA was honoring her. She gave a wonderful speech to a crowd with tears in their eyes. I might add that the emcee had a little catch in his throat during the intro. I always wondered if she was leaving the tour too soon. You see, in the second round of that event… she got a hole in one.

M

Kay Mâsak

My inspiration; my life. At the time of this writing, we have been married 48 years; we have six wonderful children, six grandchildren and two step grandchildren. So, I have a lifetime of stories I could tell you about, but I'll just share a few.

We met in 1960 at Fort Belvoir, Virginia. Her stepfather was an Army sergeant and I was there rehearsing the all Army show. One of the singers and I went over to the Post Exchange and Kay was working behind the camera counter. My friend said, "Look at that beautiful girl. I'm going to ask her out." I looked him right in the eye and said, "Not *that* girl…that's the girl I'm going to marry." He bought it. I asked her out and after convincing her that I was okay (it took a while), she agreed to a date, but *only* if we double-dated. We did.

That was April. That Christmas we were engaged and the following September, on the hottest day of the year, we were married by the Right Reverend Ferdinand Evans…and have been together ever since. She is the most courageous woman I have ever known. Our twin boys were born in two different ways in two different rooms. One was natural and one was a caesarian, an hour apart, and she was tough and ladylike through it all.

She had some major surgeries over the years and always handled them with courage and dignity. In one instance, she had a major gall bladder attack and needed surgery. There was a blockage that they couldn't clear, so after many days it was decided to remove it the old-fashioned way and they wouldn't know until they opened her up what might be in there. I was in the cold recovery room minutes after the doctor came out to tell me that she would be fine and that he found the most stones he had ever seen in one human. She was still very drowsy and weak and, I swear, her first words were, "How are the kids?"

She was honored one year as one of the ten outstanding citizens in Tarzana. Kay was always shy and quiet and certainly not a public speaker. I kept reminding her that she had to give an acceptance speech. "Want me to write one for you?" I asked. She declined and that night, her very proud family was reduced to tears, as she was brilliant. She repeated that kind of brilliance years later at my mother's wake when without my brother or me knowing about it, she got up and spoke so eloquently; a very proud moment for me and one of the reasons I love her with all my heart.

I am going to share one story now that will give you some great insight to my lady. I was asked to emcee the Navy Ball at The Beverly Wilshire Hotel — a major black-tie affair; admirals all over the place as well as the secretary of the Navy. Kay and I were seated in the back of the room with a former POW from World War II. His name is Joe Vernick. He was there in his tux, and so proud that he

was to have his POW medal pinned on him by the highest-ranking member of the Merchant Marines. After dinner, it was my turn to do my thing. I introduced dignitaries and admirals who were getting and presenting awards. After about 90 minutes and the end of the script, I was saying my good nights and people started to leave, and from the stage I see Kay rushing through the crowd toward me.

Joe Vernick with Secretary of the Navy Henry L. Garrett III.

"Get everybody back," she says. I was confused and told her that was impossible. "Honey, you have to do something. They forgot Joe Vernick and he is at the table embarrassed and crushed." I went back to him to see what we could do. He said it was supposed to be someone from the Merchant Marines. I asked him if the secretary of the Navy could do it. "Oh sure, he could, but he's too important to do that for me."

"Wait here," I said and went directly to the secretary and quickly told him the story. I asked if he would be kind enough to pin Joe's medal on him. The secretary replied, "I would be *honored*."

I said, "Wait here, sir, and I will get him."

He stopped me with, "No, I will go to him."

Not only did he go; he brought a number of admirals and staff and did a full presentation. What class. What a privilege to witness that and how proud I was and am to be married to a lady who doesn't believe in the word…can't.

Rick Monday

The first number-one draft choice in major league history, he played for the Chicago Cubs and later the Los Angeles Dodgers. I am proud to say he became a friend of mine and appears in the motivational film I wrote and directed, *Ya Gotta Believe*. Mo is now a broadcaster in the Dodger organization. But with all his athletic achievements, none stands out more than what he did on April 25, 1976.

On that day, Rick was playing centerfield for the Chicago Cubs, it was the bottom of the 4th inning and two malcontents ran into centerfield and proceeded to try to burn the American flag. Without thinking about his own safety, this six-year Marine reservist quickly ran over and swooped up the lighter-fluid-soaked flag and carried it to safety. Within minutes, the two idiots were removed from the field and, spontaneously, the crowd and the stadium rose to give Rick a standing ovation and began to sing "God Bless America." To this day, there are those, myself included, who believe that it was the greatest play in major league baseball. Way to go, Mo.

Clayton Moore

Television's The Lone Ranger. Clayton Moore was a handsome leading man in B films and Saturday serials, and then he *became* The Lone Ranger. He never smoked, drank or swore again in his life. A few years back someone decided to make a new movie about The Lone Ranger and at that point decided that Clayton Moore should no longer be allowed to wear the mask. Dumb move...and decided to take him to court to prevent it. Dumber move, as fan support swelled for him. I was hosting the MDA Telethon locally in LA and Clayton was supposed to fly in and be a guest. His flight got socked in and he wasn't going to be able to get to LA, so we did a phone patch so his fans could hear him. What a thrill. At the end of his call I told him that no matter what the outcome of the trial would be, no matter who plays the role; just as many men played Tarzan but that role will always belong to Johnny Weissmuller...he (Clayton) would *always* be The Lone Ranger. Years later when we met at the Golden Boot Awards dinner, he recalled my words and thanked me. He had given up the mask in favor of some wisely-shaped sunglasses but he couldn't fool me... he *was* The Lone Ranger.

Audie Murphy

The most decorated military man in World War II. A real hero and recipient of the Congressional Medal of Honor. I was in the last movie that Audie was in, *A Time for Dying*. Audie was playing Jesse James in Budd Boetticher's last Western. We were in Apache Junction, Arizona, and Kay was with me on location. Audie was a true gentleman and one morning, he offered Kay and me a ride to the location. Well, let me tell you something, I found out firsthand and quickly that he had nerves of steel as he was driving 100 miles

Audie Murphy with his array of medals.
PHOTO COMPLIMENTS OF
THE AUDIE MURPHY RESEARCH FOUNDATION

an hour and looking over his shoulder at us as he drove. He got us there and in one piece, I might add. If you ever get a chance to see this film, by the way, you will see one of the greatest performances by an actor I have ever seen: Victor Jory as Judge Roy Bean.

In the opening shot of the film, the young hero comes across a little scared rabbit about to be struck by a big rattlesnake. In the film the hero draws and shoots the snake. In real life, they were on the set getting ready for this shot and explaining to the man from the SPCA why we couldn't use a fake snake and if the snake is wounded what had to be done so it wouldn't suffer, etc. Unbeknownst to him, Audie was standing with the man with a real rifle, not a prop, and Budd said, "Action anytime, Audie." Audie quietly said to the man from the SPCA, "Excuse me," turned, and fired from his waist. The rattler was striking as his head disappeared from its body. A perfect shot. Audie looked back at the man and said, "He is not suffering."

My Mom…"Millie"

Don't think too much has to be said here. Every kid's hero should be his Mom and Dad. In my case my Mom was married three times…the third one was a charm that lasted. Bill Tsilivis — my Greek step father. Before she got to him though she raised two boys and worked long hours (she was one of the first

female managers of F.W. Woolworth & Co., and the first female buyer in their history). She kept us clean and fed, and taught us how to respect others, to always do our very best. I know that she was always there for our athletic events, and came to every one of my plays. She was a walking talking bundle of energy and personality. She lived in Chicago and at the age of 90 she didn't need a wheel-chair, a walker or a cane. She lived alone and was full of life right up to the day she died. I know that she was always proud of me…and me…of her.

Fred "Curly" Neal

His shaved head made him the most recognizable member of the Harlem Globetrotters basketball team. One year, a group of Hollywood stars were asked to play a charity game against them at the Fabulous Forum. It now seems hilarious to me, but the two celebrity managers we had told us as we were warming up on the court before some 15,000 people not to try to embarrass the Globetrotters, as they had to play a second game that night. *We* embarrass *them* . . . ha! We did have some pretty good athletes on our team, including Rick and David Nelson. Curley was the ball handler on the Trotters and Meadowlark Lemon was their comedy star.

Somewhere in the first half, my macho kicked in and I was able to steal the ball from Curley under their basket and had a breakaway. All I could think of as I dribbled the ball toward our basket was, "Oh my God, if I embarrassed them I will never work in this town again," and then I thought, "Please, God, don't let me miss this lay up in front of all these people." I didn't. As I headed back up the court, there were Curley and Meadowlark with their hands extended palms up and saying, "Good hands, man; good hands." I smiled and was pleased with myself and then Curley put on a dribbling exhibition. That got a standing ovation as all five members of our team *tried* to take the ball away and couldn't. He was *the best*.

Donald O'Connor

What an incredible talent. Perhaps the greatest all-around talent
the motion picture business ever produced. One of the greatest dancers in
film history. Were he just a dancer, he
would rank right up there with Gene
Kelly and Fred Astaire; were he just
a singer, he could do it with the best,
were he just a leading man, he was
handsome and deep; were he just to
do comedy he was among the best.
He and Francis the Talking Mule
saved Universal Studios from going

bankrupt years after another of my heroes, Lou Costello, and his partner, Bud
Abbott, saved it from the same fate in the '40s. But Donald could do it all —
he was a great mimic and his "Make 'Em Laugh" in *Singin' in the Rain* stands
alone as a classic piece.

We were doing a charity event in the Bay area and after the big show we
decided to do a private show for the hotel and kitchen staff. With Academy
Award-winner Art Carney at the piano (you should have heard him play ragtime),
I was introducing Donald and included the following in my intro, "When I was a
kid, my mom used to play records and the one artist your vocal timber and sound
reminded me of was Buddy Clark." When he got to the mike, he mentioned that
Buddy was one of his vocal heroes and proceeded to sing a medley of Buddy's
songs. If you had closed your eyes, you would have believed it was Buddy. Donald,
like another movie legend, Mickey Rooney, never gave a bad performance.

Shaquille O'Neal

While Shaq is a dominating force in the NBA, he is also one of the most civic-
minded individuals I ever met. Case in point: he does not play golf but he lent
his name to host a golf tournament to benefit the harbor police. While he will go

down in history as one of the top three or four centers in the history of the game, he would rather be remembered as a good citizen who is a real member of the LA Police Department. For the tourney, they made him a pair of golf shoes in his size which were later auctioned off and raised a great deal of money for the charity.

His heart is as big as his smile . . . a real Big Man.

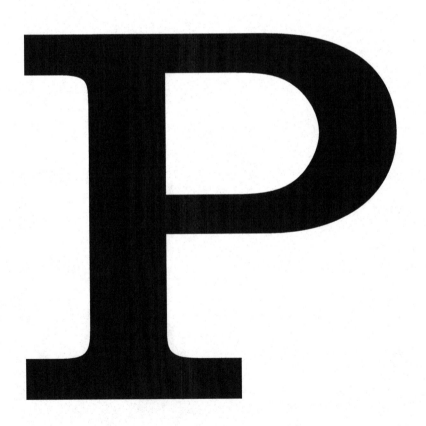

Arnold Palmer

From one king to the next. The one golfer that brought the money purses to what they are today. Television fell in love with Arnie as did his army of followers. He always challenged the course with each shot and set the bar at another level--one of the true legends of the game.

I was filming an infomercial in Florida with Payne Stewart and the cast and crew was staying at Bay Hill, Arnie's course. I had a nice suite there and loved the fact that we could walk to everything.

The day we were to film, Arnie was there playing and we were introduced. I was thrilled because when I was learning the game, I'd watch him and try to copy what he did. He really loves the game and his army. I told him that story about copying him and telling him that to this day, I putt knocked kneed and pigeon-toed like he does. Without missing a beat he said, "Yes, but your putts are going in."

A few years later, Arnie was being honored at the Jim Murray Memorial Golf Tournament, put on by Jim's widow, Linda McCoy Murray. We were out on the course and I asked Arnie if a story I had heard about him was true. The story was that a young professional golfer, Robert Damron, a protégé of Arnie's, was playing in an event at Bay Hill, as was Arnie, and Damron asked Arnie how one goes about getting invited to play in the Bob Hope Classic. Arnie explained how you have to get on a waiting list, win some big events, become well known, etc. Damron was in the group behind Arnie. And when Damron sank his first putt, there was a note in the hole saying, "You've been invited." Arnie kind of blushed and said, "Well, yes, but how in the world did you find out?" I told him that I was the sheriff, after all.

Between you and me? It was Payne who told me.

Elvis Presley

It was 1967 and I was filming *Ice Station Zebra*, and on the next soundstage they were filming *Speedway*. I was already the company clown and busy doing impressions all over the place. Someone who knew I had done Elvis on the world tour, and a friend of his, talked me into going on their set and doing my impression of Elvis...for Elvis. A little intimidating, I should say.

Those were the years of Elvis doing the fluff films: beach movies, speedway movies, etc. And as big as he was, it was a far cry from the cult worship it is now. So I went in full arctic gear, right down to thermal underwear and socks, to do my impression of Elvis for Elvis. The lovely Nancy Sinatra was his co-star and I knew Nancy but she was not on the set that day. When we were introduced, I just kind of aped whatever he was doing. He would lean on one leg, I would lean on that leg; he would hold his arm, I would hold my arm the same way; he talked about our submarine set and kind of stammered and I would answer with the same stammer. He finally asked where I was from and I told him a little town in Mississippi. He told me that's where he was from. When I told him I was from Tupelo he looked surprised, then looked at one of the smiling group and said, "I'm being had." I found him to be super polite, gracious and

fun loving. Years later, when he went back to live performing, Kay, my mom, my stepdad and I got to see him when he played The Hilton in Vegas. I did over 200 shows as Elvis in one year all over the world and it only took me watching one live performance to realize that there was only one King, and, folks, "Elvis has left the building."

Not even too many historical names begin with a "Q", although I did know the Queen of the West, Dale Evans, and the queens of country music, Reba McEntire, Dolly Parton and the Mandrells...if you'd like to count those.

R

Ronald Reagan

Before he was the President of the United States and before he was the Governor of California, Ronald Reagan was the president of the Screen Actors Guild, of which I am a member of 50 years. Right after Desert Storm, the troops and the USO were being honored at Universal Studios, and what an exiting afternoon it was. Presidents George Herbert Walker Bush, Ronald Reagan and Gerald Ford were present, along with Bob Hope and many dignitaries of that stature; generals, admirals, you name it, they were there. After the event, which was held in a cool area, we were escorted to a tented area where the photo ops were being held. When we went into President Ford's tent, we were chatting about his son, Steve, who was an actor. It was as really hot day but President Ford was bearing up well. He spoke of how much he and Betty enjoyed watching *Murder, She Wrote*.

Kay and I then were escorted to the Reagan tent. When we walked in, he said to Nancy, "Look, Mommy, it's our favorite sheriff." They were so kind and I suddenly realized that as an actor, we never know whose living rooms we are invited into. Over the years, we were in his company again and I got to know his son, Michael, and his daughter, Maureen, quite well, as we did many charity

To Ron & Kay Masak - With Very Best Wishes. Nancy Ronald Reagan

events together. When the President's health got to be too much, he asked Maureen to have me succeed him as the PSA spokesman for fire prevention. I was so honored. He was a helluva man.

Dale Robertson

Good friend Dale was a true Oklahoma cowboy and with all the movies and television shows he did, he will always be referred to as "Jim Hardy, Wells Fargo." Dale and I have played in many charity golf tournaments together and he is so much fun to be around. Prior to the Golden Boot Dinner, there is a private party given at The Sportsman's Lodge in Studio City, California. For years we had the same routine: my business partner, writer/director, Verne Nobles, Sr., and I would get there early and set up shop at the same big table by the pool. Dale and his party, who were staying at the lodge, would come and join us and we would hold court. Verne was a close friend and associate of the great western writer Louie L'Amour and he and Dale would share stories and script ideas. One by one, all the living cowboys would arrive, including the legendary stuntmen and women

and all those who created western magic in the dark theatres around the world. Dale would emcee the big dinner the following night, but they were never as much fun as the sitting around the pool. A man of great morals and patriotism, we e-mail each other often, about humor and America. He quit the starring role in a hit series because he felt some of the writing bordered on bad taste. A Man's Man I am proud to call friend.

Roy Rogers

The King of the Cowboys. As a boy who worshipped Roy and Trigger, the smartest horse in the movies, any arm of a sofa or easy chair was Trigger and I, of course, was Roy. He could ride and shoot and sing, had good manners and was good looking; traits I admired and tried to emulate in my life.

I was privileged over the years to get to know Roy and Dale and some of his family. Did some shooting (sporting clays) with Roy and his son, Dusty, and got to know his daughter, Cheryl, and her husband quite well. . Roy and Gene Autry were always honored guests at The Golden Boot Awards dinner. The thing I admired *most* about Roy was that he was exactly what I hoped he would be. He was that little boy's hero and did nothing to tarnish that memory; in fact, he enhanced it.

One year we were attending the Special Olympics at UCLA and Roy was the Honorary Chairperson that year. He was in the stands in the center of the field and each celebrity there marched with a group of Special Olympians and then joined Roy on the dais. In years past, many celebrities had the honor Roy had, but no one had the effect on those kids that Roy did. They were always

told never to break ranks but when they came around the track, they rushed to him and, God bless him, he embraced as many as he could before order was restored.

After the ceremony, as we were leaving and headed back toward the parking lot, Roy noticed out of the corner of his eye a mother pushing her son in a wheelchair, trying to catch up to him. He quietly told Dale to continue toward the car and he turned on his heel and went back to greet the mother and her son. I turned to watch Roy kneel and engage them both in conversation, give the youngster an autograph and a hug, and then quickly rejoined us. No press, no grandstanding; just a great man bringing joy to others.

Years later, when Roy passed away, we got a call from Cheryl inviting us to the funeral in Apple Valley. We accepted and it was a hot day and a beautiful ceremony attended by some of my other movie heroes. After the service, we were invited to Roy and Dale's home, where Dale told wonderful stories with us. The Queen of the West telling wonderful tales about the Happy Trails she traveled with The King of the Cowboys.

Mickey Rooney

Pound for pound, as they used to say in the fight game. "The Mick" is pound for pound as good as or better than any actor whoever lived. I have introduced him at many events and always refer to the fact that you have never seen him give a bad performance...*ever!* He has no fears about acting; whatever it is, he can do it: comedy, drama, singing, dancing, playing instruments *and* a true patriot. When he was at MGM with Gable and Tracy, Mick was the number-one box-office star worldwide. He left his career at its peak to join the military in World War II.

Every Christmas season, I emcee the Motion Picture Mothers' Christmas luncheon and the year they honored Mick and Anthony Hopkins (2005) I remarked, "How much would you pay to see these two great actors on the same screen together?" Wow!! He is the only actor in history to have been a star with

Me, Anthony Hopkins, and The Mick.

three different names. In vaudeville, he was Joe Yule, Jr. His dad was vaudeville star Joe Yule, Sr., who starred in the *Maggie and Jiggs* movies. He then did a series of comedies as Mickey (Hisself) McGuire and finally Mickey Rooney. He has been a star all his life, starting in films in the '20s and still making movies today. Though only 5'3" tall, he is a Giant talent.

S

Alan Shepard

For those of you who saw the movie *The Right Stuff*, Alan Shepard was the astronaut that was always doing his impression of Bill Dana's Jose Jimenez. One of the original 7; when he got his turn to go to the moon he would make the most of it. He will forever be known as the man who hit the golf ball on the moon.

We were doing a celebrity golf tournament in the bay area and he and I were having breakfast one morning when a young, college-aged man approached and said, "Excuse me, Admiral Shepard, but you're the astronaut who hit the golf ball on the moon, aren't you?" When he said, "Yes," he readied himself for the following question he had become accustomed to: "What ball did you hit?" He never told anyone what kind of a ball he hit, because every manufacturer sent him theirs!!! Instead, the young man asked, "Tell me something, sir. Did they ever find the ball you hit?" After a short pause I looked up at this guy and said, "THEY???" From his quizzical look and Alan's laughter, I continued. "They, who? There were two people up there and he hit the ball over two miles." Shepard was on the floor...I mean, *really* on the floor, holding his sides with laughter. He told me he was going to steal that story and not give me credit, but I heard later that...he did. Both stole the story...but gave me credit.

Frank Sinatra

The Chairman of the Board, Ol' Blue Eyes. Kay and I had the opportunity to
see Mr. Sinatra open many times, including the night his mother was killed in
a plane crash. The greatest interpreter of a lyric in music history and a defender
of civil rights *long* before it became the law of the land. I have played in his golf

To Kay and Ron —
with my very best
wishes —
Frank Sinatra
'95

tournament benefiting the Barbara Sinatra Children's Center in Rancho Mirage, California for 20 years.

The first time we met one-on-one was in Tommy Lasorda's office at Dodger Stadium. Mr. Sinatra was a season ticket holder from the day the Dodgers arrived in LA. His seats were right over the first base dugout. He and Tommy became

close friends. Tommy was introduced to Frank's Vegas audience the night his mother perished. But the first time we spoke was in Tommy's office. We were alone and he was deep in thought. It was the day his good friend Bing Crosby had died in Spain. When Mr. S. sighed and came out of his deep thought he said, "I was trying to think of Bing's life…don't think he ever had an enemy, don't think he ever said anything political, and now his body is being held in Spain. Maybe I should just stay in the desert and not travel."

A story I have told often about Mr. S is this: One year, the team I played on in the Frank Sinatra Golf Tournament was fortunate enough to win. At the private after party at Frank's place I was sitting with Kay and baseball greats Freddy Lynn and Ralph Kiner. Frank and Barbara were sitting across the way with members of my team from Capitol Records and Nancy and Larry Manetti (Rick from *Magnum, P.I.*). Larry and Nancy were dear friends of Frank's for years.

Larry kept gesturing for me to come over to the table but I declined as I could see that Frank did not really want to be there. His look was that of a man who

would rather be in his robe and slippers than sitting there in a tux. Larry kept gesturing and finally Kay said, "You had better go over there or the Sinatras will think
you are being rude." So, over I went. I said my hellos to Nancy and Larry, then paid
my respects to Barbara. As I was getting ready to leave, I caught Frank's eye and
nodded to him; he responded with a smile and put his hand to his mouth and threw
me that famous Sinatra kiss. When I got back to our table, Kay asked me what happened and I told her. When she asked if I spoke with Frank, I told her, "No, but I
nodded, he smiled and threw me a kiss." She laughed and said, "Sure. He probably
thought you were Shecky." (Shecky Greene, one of the world's great comedy stars.)
Kay can really be funny at times. She broke up our table…at my expense.

Robert Stack

One of the real good guys. We became good buddies over the years and
attended many shooting events (he was a world-class shot) and golf tournaments
together. We shot sporting clays all over the country: Dana Pointe for the Charlton Heston Celebrity Shoots, Tennessee for Louise Mandrell's Shoots and he shot
with me when I was asked to co-host, with Leslie Easterbrook, the first Hollywood Celebrity shoot. He was such a legend in the shooting field that when the
Nemacolin Woodlands Resort & Spa were building a new $4,000,000 Sporting

Clays Academy, the owner chartered a plane from publishing mogul and shooter Bob Peterson to fly us to Pennsylvania. Bob and Rosemarie and their daughter, Elizabeth, and Kay and I flew out to christen the Sporting Clays Academy. It is a beautiful place and the Academy, designed by Mike Daveys (who designed one for the British royal family), is like shooting into a beautiful painting at each shooting stand. Other celebrity shooters joined us there and we had a marvelous time. There was no *Unsolved Mystery* about Robert Stack. He told Hollywood stories with the best of them. He lived a lot of them and this handsome man enjoyed nothing more than telling a joke. Again, I say, he was one of the really Good Guys.

Gloria and James Stewart.

James Stewart

General Jimmy Stewart, another great American, who enlisted at the top of his career to serve a nation under fire. I was honored to represent *Murder, She Wrote* at the Grand Opening of the Universal Studios in Florida. They were bringing 50 celebrities and all three networks for the grand opening, and the list, except for me, read like the Who's Who of Hollywood: James Stewart, Charlton Heston, Ernest Borgnine, Bill Cosby, Sylvester Stallone, Michael J. Fox, Janet Leigh, Walter Lantz (creator of Woody Woodpecker), Hanna and Barbera,

Robert Wagner, Jill St. John, Anthony Perkins, Steven Spielberg and the like. We were on chartered flights and Kay and I were on the one with Alfred Hitchcock's daughter Patricia, Janet Leigh, Ernie Borgnine (with whom I did my first movie and who is *always* so gracious), Charlton Heston and James Stewart, along with many dignitaries from Universal and the press. Jimmy boarded first and when I was going by the flight deck door, the captain leaned out and said, "Hey, Sheriff, ask the General if he'd like to check out the flight deck."

So as I passed the Stewarts, I said to Jimmy, "The Captain asked me to ask you if you would like to go up there and take this baby off."

And he said, as only he could, "Well, uh gee…Th Th That, uh, that sounds swell." A few minutes later he went up there and *did* stay in there with the captain as we took off. Now whether it was him or not I can't swear to, but … ???

Unbeknownst to any of us up in the air, as we were coming into Florida there was an electrical storm going on below us. We circled for a time and when we landed there were hundreds of reporters there as R.J. Wagner and Jill greeted us. A reporter stuck a microphone in my face and asked if we were frightened up there during the storm. I said, "Why would I be frightened? I was with a pilot in Stewart, and if we had to ditch in the water, we had McHale in Borgnine, and if that didn't work, we had Moses who could part the sea, so we felt safe." What a great memory that time was.

Payne Stewart

Right before his untimely death, Payne and I did an infomercial for a golf product. This was my first meeting with my friend and business partner, Verne Nobles, Sr., who hired me unseen on a golf course to do the infomercial. I was playing golf at Lakeside CC with America's number-one DJ, Rick Dees, when I got a call from a lady who told me that golf photographer Paul Lester had recommended me highly and asked if I could leave Friday for Florida. I could and did.

We stayed at and filmed at Arnold Palmer's Bay Hill Country Club. I was told not to worry about the script, as it would all be on a TelePrompTer. On the flight from LA to Florida, I *did* study the written script. The shoot day was going to be the only day we would have Payne as he had to leave the next morning for the tour. I started filming and Payne was to join us later that morning. The sky started to look like rain would be coming and we might be in trouble. Verne, who is a wonderful director, saw the problem coming as Payne came out of the clubhouse and into a cart that was ready for him with a walkie-talkie. Verne told Payne that the camera was rolling and to just drive up to the tee box, tee it up

Statue commemorating Stewart's win in the 1999 U.S. Open.

and hit it as close to the pin as he could (told you Verne didn't know that much about golf). Payne did just that; drove up to the tee and proceeded to lay his shot three feet from the pin. "Cut, print, next shot."

We set up down at the green where our shots landed and started to ad-lib, as there was *no* TelePrompTer. All of a sudden a light rain started to fall and everyone started getting concerned. Verne told them to keep filming until our shirts looked wet, as the rain was not being picked up on film. Then it came. God bless Payne as he told Verne that he had an indoor putting green in his home and volunteered it for the shoot. What a classy champion.

When people who know that I worked with him ask me what he was like, I tell two stories to show the character and humor of the man. As we were approaching the front of his beautiful home, I remarked that the ornate staircase outside looked like the entrance to the castle in *Beauty and the Beast*. Without missing a beat, he said, "It is. Come on, *Beast*."

As we sat and began filming the next sequence in his indoor putting room, because of the sound, we could not have the air conditioning running in the room. Florida: humid…muggy…HOT!!! But he was a magnificent trooper. I looked around the room at many different colored golf bags and wonderful photos on the wall and asked him if any meant more than any other. Again, without missing a beat, he pointed to a photo of himself and an older gentleman and said, "Right before he died, we won a father/son tournament." The golf world misses Payne Stewart…and so do I.

General Norman Schwarzkopf

Stormin' Norman — The General who led our troops to victory in Desert Storm. As long as we are talking sporting clays, let's stay with it on this story. We were doing a celebrity shoot at The Homestead in Virginia, not long after the war. I am an early riser, as is the General, so we would meet for breakfast early and then stay around for coffee as the others would join us. He shared some wonderful stories with me, some personal, some historical. I told him that he was so popular back here that if he wanted he probably could be President of the United States. He informed me that offers were made to be on the ticket from both parties. I asked if he regretted saying no. He said, "Ron, most of this country thinks I did a pretty good job over there — why would I want half of them to dislike me? We now live in a tabloid journalistic world where the media will spend two years building you up and praising you so that they can spend the next four years tearing you down. During the conflict, President [George H.W.] Bush had the highest popularity rating in history and now he is fighting for his political life." He was right.

All the celebrities lead their own team; 12 teams moving from stand to stand. I have never been called "Whispering Ron," so as we approached the General's team, he was shooting and as he missed his first target he shot me a look and said, "Mâsak, I can hear your voice all over the mountain." I replied, "General, that's the way I want it. That's live ammo and I want you to be aware of where I am at all times." He smiled.

The next day we were shooting and again we came upon a stand where the General was shooting and had not missed. This time I was as quiet as a mouse

but I must have been on his mind, for on the next "Pull" he missed a shot and immediately shot me a look. I smiled, closed my fist and said to him, "Gotcha."

That night I emceed the dinner and had the honor of introducing him. I remember saying that this man was the real-life hero that John Wayne portrayed in the movies. I told the audience that I would follow him into Hell because I knew he would bring us back. When he took the mike he said some nice things, but in my case he would think twice about getting me out of Hell! I can always tell my grandchildren that this wonderful General would drive a drafted MP around Virginia in a Range Rover. Over the years we have done events together like The Safari Club International Convention. He, former President Bush and I spent some quality time together. They are two very classy gentlemen and I am proud to have on my wall a photo of the General, who inscribed it, "To Ron Mâsak...The Best and LOUDEST MP ever."

Danny Thomas

As a kid, I was a big fan of Danny Thomas. He was such a versatile performer. He could sing, so stand-up comedy and it was in Chicago where he emerged into a nightclub headliner.

When he went to Hollywood to act in movies and finally television in *Make Room for Daddy*, he embodied every thing I admired in a star. He had a large nose but refused to buckle to the studio's wishes to have a nose job and still became a romantic lead opposite such beauties as Doris Day. He, along with his business partner, Sheldon Leonard, created *The Dick Van Dyke Show* and *The Andy Griffith Show*. I so admired the fact that it was family and God that were the real important things in his life. When he was down at his lowest, he made a vow to St. Jude that if he were ever to become successful, he would build a shrine to St. Jude. In 1962 he dedicated his shrine, The St. Jude's Children's Research Hospital, in Memphis, Tennessee. He lived his life by believing, "Success has nothing to do with what you gain in life or accomplish for yourself. It's what you do for others."

Danny Thomas with Angela Cartwright.

U

Two of my Heroes...Johnny Unitis and my son Mike.

Johnny Unitas

Arguably the greatest quarterback in the history of the NFL. His record of throwing a touchdown pass in 47 consecutive games may never be broken. This legend, in his high-top cleats and crew cut who was an all-time great in the violent world of football, was a quiet and gentle man who gave of his time and talents to many charities. The one where I would see him most was at the American Airlines Celebrity Golf tournament benefiting the Susan G. Koman Breast Cancer Research. He was a humble hero who stood head and shoulders above his peers. I do know this: he had a great laugh and seemed to enjoy my humor at these events. His football records stand for themselves as will his humanitarian efforts. Johnny U will always be remembered and he has forever set the bar for NFL Quarterbacks.

Renée Valente

This one-time head of Screen Gems casting and major producer at 20th Century-Fox is the classy lady responsible for discovering Burt Reynolds and Academy Award-winner Anthony Hopkins. She found Hopkins in Europe for the project *QB VII* and told the network (who wasn't sure), "If you don't trust my

judgment then you can have my job. *This* is the actor for that role." Thank God they kept her and hired him for the role. He was brilliant.

I was the LA host of the Jerry Lewis MDA telethon for many years and I asked her to produce it locally for me one year. She did. That year we had more stars for our cutaways than Jerry had in Las Vegas. To just name a few, we had

Emmy winner Renée Valente.

most of the LA Dodgers, Regis Philbin, Victoria Principal, Kate Jackson, Patty Duke and John Astin. She came to work with both barrels blazing and stayed up the whole time I was on the air. She had some of the most powerful casting directors helping out and I'm forever grateful to her for donating her time and talent as well as a check to MDA.

W

Lew Wasserman

The last of the big studio moguls. Mr. Wasserman *was* MCA Universal. Feared by many; respected by all. When they opened The Universal Studios in Florida, I was asked to represent *Murder, She Wrote* as Angela was out of the country. We were treated royally. Kay, our youngest, Christine, and I had our own villa, a

white chauffeured limo and all the perks. On the actual day of the grand opening, all of the executives and dignitaries had one of the 50 "celebrities" assigned to them. I was blessed to spend the day with the Wasserman family. We were to try all the rides and events and do interviews about them to the press. Mr. W. was so aware of that and made sure that his family was afforded the front-of-the-line perks, but he chose *not* to do that. Instead, he would go in the back way and meet us — a helluva man.

My professional partner, writer/director Verne Nobles, Sr., and I would have many business lunches at The Universal Grill, and Mr. Wasserman was always there at his table in the back of the room and our table was always next to his. He was always early, as were Verne and I, so at least twice a week we would visit before his or our guests would arrive. He would regale us with stories of the stars and films he was responsible for, yet he chose *never* to have his name on the screen credits.

I used to see him and his family at Dodger Stadium a lot as well. They were season ticket holders. Two quick stories come to mind. The last time the actors went on strike, I said to him, "Hey, Papa, why don't you end this strike as you did all the others in the past?" He answered, "No one asked me." Now he was always used to my humor but saw that I wasn't kidding this time when I said, "You will hear from SAG this afternoon." I called President William Daniels' office. That afternoon a meeting was set up with Mr. Wasserman and three days later the strike was over. I later asked him what he told them. He said, "The best way to get on with negotiations is to throw all the lawyers out of the room. Have the two negotiators sit and talk and *don't feed them* until it's settled."

The other story that I love happened during the 2000 presidential elections, with the now-famous counting of the chads in Florida and the Supreme Court decisions. He loved politics and I loved law, so every day we would discuss what was going on. Over the years, Mr. W. had many presidents stay at his home, was a major contributor to the Democratic Party and would host fundraisers. One day I walked in and he said, "Well, they are counting again." I said, "It's over. The Supreme Court will stop it." He said, "The Supreme Court won't touch it again." As we know, they did and stopped all the fuss. The next day I come in and he called me to his table and said, "Mâsak, I have contributed millions to the Democratic Party, I have hosted fundraisers and had Presidents sleeping under my roof. I will never contribute another dime." I said, "Why, may I ask?" His reply, "Because, Mâsak, if the sheriff from a fictitious little town in Maine can be right…I must have been wrong all those years." We both shared a great laugh. I miss him…so does our industry.

John Wayne

The Duke: The one movie star above all who was bigger than life. A winner of the Academy Award, he always said, "I don't act, I react," and he did that longer and better than most. He played soldiers, sailors, marines, pilots, detectives, longshoremen and historical figures. He produced; he directed; he was always in the top-ten box office, and movie and television stars melted when they met him. He'd always greet the new stars with, "Let's do a picture together, kid."

I was asked early on in my Hollywood career to emcee the Stuntman's Ball honoring John Wayne. I jumped at the chance. Kay and I sat at the next table from Duke and got to observe him all night. He was a Man's Man, all right, and, again, bigger than life. He was a two-fisted drinker, but was in control and that big friendly smile was so evident all night.

Over the years we got to know the rest of his family, doing many events with Michael, Patrick and other members of the family. But one night I remember

almost word for word. The great comedian Foster Brooks was on the bill. He was unknown at the time and Duke had never seen him, so when I introduced Foster as "A former president of the Stuntman's Association" and he went into his slightly inebriated act, Duke started to feel for this poor soul. He suddenly got it when Foster said, "My wife told me to be sure to check my fly before coming out here, but I told her not to worry because…dead men don't fall out windows." Duke sprayed his drink and let out with that great laugh of his and sat back and enjoyed the rest of Foster's act.

When it came time to receive his award, I remember so clearly that he walked to center stage, as *only* John Wayne could walk, stood there holding the award for a minute and finally said, "Well, I want to thank you for this. I watched a lot of you grow up in this business. Hell, I watched a lot of your *fathers* grow up in this business. Over the years I have said a lot of things about stuntmen…never anything to your back and never anything you'd be ashamed of. Thank you and goodnight." He left the stage and all that was missing was someone whistling the theme from *The High and the Mighty*.

I almost got to work with him in his last movie, *The Shootist*, but it didn't pan out. But there he was in his 70s with one lung and half a stomach and with the cancer that would eventually claim him. He was playing a gunfighter dying of cancer, taking on three bad guys and winning…and you still believed he could do it.

There was only one Duke. He will never be forgotten.

David Wolper

Another giant in the entertainment industry. One of the great producers of all time: *Roots, Willy Wonka and the Chocolate Factory,* and *The Thorn Birds,* to name just a few. He was awarded the Jean Hersholt Award at the Academy Awards. He had a beautiful home in the Napa Valley and hosted two major events: a golf tournament benefiting The Boys and Girls Clubs and a private tournament at his home. He had a 9-hole golf course with two different tee boxes so it played like 18, and for those who did not play golf he had a fashionable croquet game. The great thing about the private tournament was your teammates. He invited the cream of the industry, the likes of which included Jack Valenti, Johnny Mathis,

Joe DiMaggio, Digger Phelps, Richard Crenna, Peter Uberoff, Rick Barry, Elgin Baylor, Dick Smothers, Clint Eastwood. My team was fortunate enough to win and that trophy has a place of honor in our home. The last event would be an elimination shootout where the player was only allowed one club. The finals came down to Rick Barry and me, with the Who's Who of Hollywood watching us. I laid a long putt next to the hole and Rick, who was one of the greatest shooters in the NBA, put his long putt in. He won but I had the most fun.

Mr. Wolper also produced the opening and closing of the Olympics in Los Angeles and did a masterful job. Kay and I were honored to be a part of his events. He once said, "A producer is a person who dreams. Good producers make dreams come true." He did just that.

X

Bob, Kathy, Christine, Debbie, Tami, and Mike stand behind Kay and Me.

X-Factor

Although I did eat at Xavier Cugat's restaurant once…and met stuntman/ actor X. Brands, I have reserved this spot for my family as they are the X-Factor in my life. When I was a young dreamer and knew what I wanted to do for a living, I was sure it would not be fair to fall in love with someone and subject them to a struggling actor's life. So I never dreamed of a family life. Well, I dreamed it but never thought it could happen. I have already written how I met Kay and she gave me six beautiful children, four daughters: Tammy, Debbie, Kathy, and Chrissy, and twin boys, Mike and Bob. They, along with our Grandchildren, are my life. I have always told people that I was not a wealthy man, but I was the richest man on earth for I had the love and respect of a beautiful family. They have given me more joy than any man deserves. We have traveled all over the world together and I have been proud of every moment I have spent with them.

Kay has inspired me to heights I never knew were possible. She is my inspiration. She has inspired a poem out of me every Sunday for over 40 years. Those poems have become sort of a diary of our life together. God has blessed us. I can honestly say that I wouldn't trade places with any man on earth; therefore, in the X-Factor tone, I decided that I would never do anything in my career that would embarrass my family. So, I never did any nude shots in film and so far no vulgar language and I myself am kind of proud of that. I was once going to write a book entitled *I Make Everyone Laugh But My Wife*. I probably should include some of my kids in that title, but I *do* make them smile a lot.

General Chuck Yeager

Perhaps the greatest pilot who-ever lived, General Yeager is his own man. The supreme test pilot and the first man to break the sound barrier. He is a *true* American. In World War II, he flew 64 combat missions, downed 13 enemy planes, including five in one day. He is a true hero in every sense of the word and was a subject in the best-selling novel and movie *The Right Stuff.*

The first time I met the General was at a function honoring General Jimmy Doolittle. It was right after the Dodgers had won the World Series and some of them had put out a record of *We Are the Champions.* Dodger catcher Steve Yeager had never met his blood relative and I introduced them to each other and the General told Steve, "Ain't no Yeager ever could sing worth a damn and you are sure as hell proving it." Over the years I got to know the General a little better and when I emceed the Safari Club Dinner I had the General, Stormin' Norman and President Bush at one time. What made Chuck stand out was that he was his own man. We were all in nice tuxes…the difference was Chuck wore a tux jacket and blue jeans.

The next day we were both doing a radio interview and I listened carefully to his words like "No landing you can walk away from is ever bad." When asked how many times as a test pilot he crashed, he said, "Does that include helicop-ters?" He talked statistics like, "Over 80% of the enemy is shot down by 11% of the pilots and those 11% had one thing in common; they were all country boys." When I asked why he felt that was, he replied, "Country boys know when to back off and wait for another opportunity and they were all hunters and could gauge windage." Interesting, huh? So is General Chuck Yeager.

Steve Yeager

Co-MVP of the 1981 World Series/former catcher for the Los Angeles Dodgers, who caused a stir by posing nude for *Playgirl*. He created the concept for the catcher's mask throat protector after having had his neck pierced by a broken bat. I first met Steve when he, Garvey and Davey Lopes appeared in a television pilot

Boomer and the guy he taught to catch well enough to do it for 33 years for Hollywood Stars.

I hosted, *Hey Coach*. I got to know him really well while working out with the Dodgers and we became like brothers. He even bought the house across the street from me and lived there for a year while he was building another. Steve hosted a golf tournament and *all* the celebrities wanted to play in that one. He would drive some of us to the event in a huge motor home — always smiling and outgoing and giving. He was a 4-letter man in high school and yet would always, when speaking to the kids, encourage them to stay in school and get an education.

He had a Jacuzzi in his front yard and when Big Boog Powell was traded to the Dodgers, Steve invited Boog to Steve's place. This was still in my youth and my drinking days so Steve called me up to come over and meet Boog. I threw on a warm-up suit and went over and there was Boog on the Jacuzzi, with a drink in his hand that was the size of the dispenser you'd make a malted milkshake in. When we were introduced, he offered me some of his drink...powerful. Three hours later, we were all in the Jacuzzi and I told them it was time for me to head home so I asked Steve where my warm-up suit was. He said, "You are wearing it." Haven't had a drink now in over 20 years — ha ha.

Robert Young

One of my childhood heroes, as he always reminded me of my Uncle Harold, long before he dispensed fatherly advice on *Father Knows Best*. I finally got to meet him when we did a two-part *Marcus Welby/Owen Marshall* together. I was so impressed with his work ethic and his professionalism. He was very kind to the new kid in town and when the filming was finished he actually sent me a note thanking me...can you imagine how thrilled I was? Many years later when Mr. Young was 90, one of his friends who knew me as well told me that Mr. Young was getting depressed, and gave me his address. So, I wrote to him and reminded him of his kindness to me and thanked him for showing me how the real stars treat the newcomers. He wrote back and thanked me and told me that one of his friends gave him a pillow cover that read, "Growing old isn't bad...It's S—T." I am so happy we can still see his work on television. He was a class act.

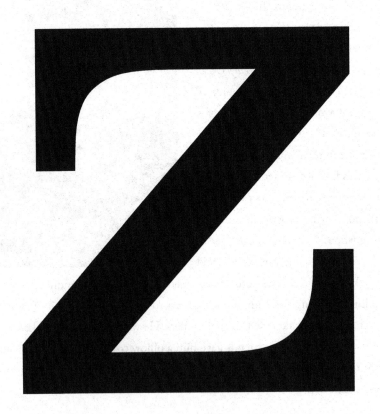

Tony Zale

Former middleweight champion of the world and most famous for his three fights with Rocky Graziano. He was known as "The Man of Steele" or "The Gary Steel Man." I did some boxing in Chicago and was selected to represent The Image of the Golden Gloves at a dinner honoring sports writer Arch Ward, who founded the All-Star Baseball game, The College Pro All-Star Game and many other sporting ventures we now take for granted.

Back to Tony Zale. I was doing some boxing for the CYO and Johnny Baer, who was Tony's corner man, was our coach. Tony used to come and visit. I was in the ring and my opponent didn't show, so Johnny said, "Stay here. Tony wants to work out a little and he will show you a few things." I weighed about 174 lbs. and thought I was pretty good and, holy cow, I will be in the ring with the former middleweight champion of the world! He came in and I told him not to hurt me. He smiled and said, "No problem. I will pull all my punches." I was a little cocky because I had never been knocked down in the ring. The bell rang and I came out and threw three quick jabs that connected.

He threw a short right, six inches at the most, and I was on my ass sitting on the floor in the corner of the ring. I heard birds and I thought my brain had separated from my skull because I could hear clicking when I turned. There was Tony in my face as I was pulling off the gloves and I said to him, "I thought you said you were going to pull your punches?" He said, "I *did*."

These are just *some* of my heroes from A-Z, along with every firefighter, law enforcement officer, teacher, and all the men and women who serve and defend this nation. There are hundreds more stories and, who knows…if you like, I may just tell you some more of them.

About The Author

Ron Mâsak (MAY-SACK) was born in Chicago, Illinois, the son of a salesman/musician (Floyd L.), and a mother (Mildred), who was a merchandise buyer. Ron attended Chicago City College, and studied theater at both the CCC and the Drama Guild. He made his acting debut with the Drama Guild in Chicago in *Stalag 17* in 1954.

Since he was seen by millions of households worldwide, starring as Sheriff Mort Metzger in the hit television series *Murder, She Wrote,* and given that he has also been seen and heard in hundreds of television and radio Commercials (he was named, "King of Commercials" by Hollywood columnist James Bacon) and since he has starred in 20 feature films and guest starred in some 350 TV shows, it is no wonder that he is often introduced as one of America's most familiar faces.

Trained in the classics, Ron has proven to be equally at home on stage or screen with Shakespeare or slapstick. He has played everything from Stanley in *A Streetcar Named Desire* and Sakini in *Teahouse of the August Moon* to Will Stockdale in *No Time For Sergeants* and Antony in *Julius Caesar.* As more proof of his versatility, in one production of *Mr. Roberts,* he played Ensign Pulver and in another he portrayed Mr. Roberts himself. In his hometown of Chicago, Ron was resident leading man at The Candlelight Dinner Playhouse from 1962 to 1966, never missing a single performance. As with many performers, it was the Army that provided Ron with a platform from which to display his all-around talents for performing, writing and directing. In 1960-61, Ron toured the world doing vocal impressions in the all-Army show entitled *Rolling Along.* Once again, he never missed a show.

Never one to be pigeonholed, Ron continued to demonstrate his incredible range of talent in such films as *Ice Station Zebra, Daddy's Gone A-Hunting, Tora! Tora! Tora!, Evel Knievel, A Time For Dying, Harper Valley PTA, Cops & Roberts* and *The Man From Clover Grove*. It was during Clover Grove that Ron added credits as a lyric writer, as he wrote and sang the title song. He played his first big screen villain starring in *No Code of Conduct*. Among his many television roles, he starred as Charley Wilson in his own summer series, *Love Thy Neighbor,* Count Dracula on *The Monkees* and was submitted for an Emmy nomination for one of his ten starring roles on *Police Story*. He's been seen on *Magnum P.I., Webster* and *Columbo*. His movies of the week include *The Neighborhood, In the Glitter Palace, Pleasure Cove, Once An Eagle, The Law and Harry McGraw* and Robert Altman's *Nightmare in Chicago*.

Ron's variety work includes emceeing hundreds of shows for, among others, Kenny Rogers, Diahann Carroll, Alabama, Billy Crystal, The Steve Garvey Classics, Tony Orlando, The Lennon Sisters, Trini Lopez, Connie Stevens, Billy Davis and Marilyn McCoo, The Michael Landon Classics and The Beau Bridges Classics.

Ron is also considered to be the most famous salesman since Willy Loman, as he starred in the four most successful sales motivational films of all time: *Second Effort* with Vince Lombardi, *Time Management* with James Whitmore, *How to Control Your Time* with Burgess Meredith and *Ya Gotta Believe* with Tommy Lasorda, which Ron wrote and directed. He is a sought after motivational speaker. He has traveled allover the country as spokesman for a major brewing company and for 15 years was the voice of the Vlasic Pickle stork. Ron played Lou Costello in commercials for Bran News, McDonald's, and Tropicana Orange Juice.

Frequently seen on the talk and game show circuit, Ron has been a celebrity panelist on such game shows as *Password, Tattletales, Crosswits, Liar's Club, Showoffs* and *Match Game*. He was a regular panelist on *To Tell The Truth*.

Ron's private life is also one of varied interests and talents, devoting time and energy working with many charities. For eight years he was the LA host for the *Jerry Lewis Telethon* and recipient of MDA's first Humanitarian of the Year Award. He has served as field announcer for the Special Olympics in support of Special Needs children, and was named Man of the Year by Volunteers

Assisting Cancer Stricken Families. In addition, he contributes much time to work with Multiple Sclerosis, Cystic Fibrosis, Breast Cancer Awareness and hosts charity golf tournaments for among others, Childhelp USA, for whom he is a worldwide ambassador.

Relaxation for Ron includes time spent with friends on the golf course, tennis court, baseball diamond, ski slopes or at Dodger Stadium. A fine athlete, Ron was once offered a professional baseball contract with The Chicago White Sox.

Future projects include Ron starring as Mark Twain in the feature film, *Mark Twain's Greatest Adventure*, which he will co-produce, and a one-man show he wrote on Twain called *At Home with Mark Twain*.

Ron's favorite role remains that of husband to his lovely wife Kay, and father to their six children as well as grandfather to their six grandchildren (and two step grandchildren). They reside in Tarzana, California, where Ron has served for 35 years as, of course, its honorary sheriff.

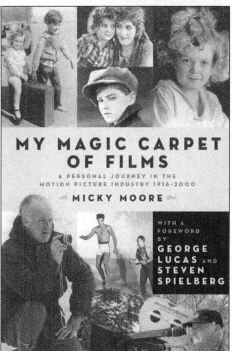

CPSIA information can be obtained
at www.ICGtesting.com
Printed in the USA
FSOW04n1140150716
22793FS

9 781593 935108